"Michael has a long and distinguished history at Microsoft, leading product and engineering organizations serving the world's customers. In his book he shares an outlook on corporate life developed along the way, starting from an immigrant escaping tyranny through his professional ascent during hyper-growth, right up until challenges of the pandemic. While sharing his personal experiences, he brings forth lessons and outlook that serve a broader audience."

— Steven Sinofsky, former Microsoft Executive

"A short, effective read that is authentic and reflects your experiences and learnings through your life and your career. Interweaving the book with a set of personal examples, anecdotes, and stories makes for an interesting, yet thought-provoking read. It is a good collection of dos and don'ts, as far as finding your balance to be productive, successful, and happy."

— Soma Somasegar, Managing Director at Madrona Venture Group

"It's a quick and easy read. Michael draws from his own unique experiences to create a handbook for surviving in corporate America."

— Babak Parviz, Vice President at Amazon

"It isn't easy to prepare a college student for the corporate world. Michael's experiences reveal what's difficult to teach, but crucial to know. By understanding what to expect, young talents can prevent failure and gain insights that could otherwise take decades to discover."

— Dr. Payman Arabshahi, Associate Chair—Industry Liaison, University of Washington, Department of Electrical and Computer Engineering

"Michael is a seasoned storyteller who shares experiences in how to build a successful mindset in corporate America. Michael provides an honest assessment in how to create a balanced outlook that can find harmony among diverse opinions while standing up to discrimination."

— Craig Fleischman, former Microsoft Executive

"Valuable reading for those seeking new strategies to guide their businesses and communities as we emerge from the pandemic, changed and each hoping to make those changes turn out for the better."

— Mike Flynn, Retired Publisher of Puget Sound Business Journal

...I'M TIRED

HOW TO SURVIVE AND SUCCEED IN CORPORATE AMERICA

AVIVA
PUBLISHING
New York

MICHAEL NASSIRIAN

I'm Tired: How to Survive & Succeed In Corporate America
Copyright @2020 by Michael Nassirian

Hardcover ISBN: 978-1-63618-028-1
ePub ISBN: 978-1-63618-029-8
Library of Congress Control Number: 2020922853

Editor: Erin Donley Communication
Cover & Interior Design: Fusion Creative Works, fusioncw.com

Every attempt has been made to properly source all quotes and attribute all research.

Published by Aviva Publishing
Lake Placid, NY
518-523-1320
www.avivapubs.com

AVIVA
PUBLISHING
New York

Printed in the United States of America

First Edition

CONTENTS

...I'M TIRED

Thanks to my wife Neda and my son and daughter
Baabak and Ava for helping me shape my career,
for coping through all my challenges and
offering their support along the way.

You are the love of my life.

PROLOGUE

One story can alter the course of your life.

I heard a parable early in my career that's lingered with me for over 40 years. When it was told to me as a young man, it didn't have a significant impact, yet through my years in Corporate America, it would drift back into my thoughts and serve as a stern reminder of my values. If just *one* part of this book sticks with you, let it be the lesson of this story. It's been told by others in various ways. This is the version that has guided me to live my best life:

A wealthy and successful American businessman took his family on an island vacation. He awoke early one morning for a stroll on the beach and found a fisherman getting out of a small boat holding one large fish. Businessman asked, "What is that?" Fisherman replied, "It's my catch of the day." "What will you do with it?" "I'm headed to the market to sell it." "And what will you do with the money?" Businessman inquired. Fisherman explained, "Well, I'm going to buy some food, go home, have breakfast with my wife, then maybe have a rest."

Businessman was further intrigued. "Then what?" "Well, I'll take a walk on the beach with my wife and have a relaxing conversation, while enjoying the nice walk." "Then what?" "Well, I'll probably gather with my buddies, have lunch, take a brisk walk, then siesta." "Then what?" "We'll gather with friends and family, have a good dinner with laughs and drinks." "Then what?" "We'll go to sleep. Then, I'll wake up early in the morning and do it again."

Businessman said, "Listen, I've been working in a corporate environment for a long time and have been extremely successful. Let me help you do the same. Starting tomorrow at sea, stay a little longer." Fisherman was confused. "Why?" "Instead of one fish, you get two fish, which gives you more to sell at the market and more money to save."

Fisherman responded, "Then what?" "The next day, you stay even longer to get more fish, more money, and more savings." "Then what?" "You'll be able to buy a bigger boat for deep sea fishing." "Then what?" "Well, deep sea fishing will give you

*bigger and better fish, so you can make even more money."
"Then what?" "You'll buy additional boats and hire fishermen
to operate them. Eventually, you'll have five, 10, 20 boats, and
a full staff of people working for you." "Then what?"*

*"In 15-20 years, when you have a whole fleet of boats and
employees, you'll be able to retire. That's when you can spend as
much time as you want with your wife. You can go for walks,
enjoy meals together, relax when you feel like it, and spend time
with friends and family."*

*Fisherman didn't say a word. He just looked puzzled at
Businessman. That's when Businessman had an epiphany. He
realized what he was preaching to Fisherman is what he was
currently doing. The life he portrayed for himself in 15-20 years
was happening today. Businessman thanked him for listening
and continued his walk on the beach. All day, he thought about
his life and envied Fisherman.*

In this story, I saw myself as the fisherman. He didn't have
to think twice when declining the businessman's offer. His
life already contained all the benefits that were promised.
Why should he wait until retirement to enjoy the important
things in life--family, excitement, and the people he loved.

When I'd be striving hard at work, losing sleep, skipping exercise, or missing friends and family, the fisherman's reflection would appear in the mirror urging me to seek balance. That guy wanted a life of his choosing. His day had variety. His time was balanced. His work was just one aspect of having a rich life, not the majority of it. His success wasn't measured in dollars and gain, but rather in the quality and fullness of his life.

Who do you want to be in the story? The choice is yours.

INTRODUCTION

In early March 2020, after participating in a series of business and fundraising events, I got hit with body aches and a debilitating cough. I had just started writing this book as my yearly goal, but before I could type a word, I was flattened with what felt like the worst flu ever. There wasn't a fever, as far as I could tell, and no sore throat, but the tightness in my chest squeezed like a vice. When I tried to speak, a coughing fit would ensue. It was as though I was gasping for air in the middle of the ocean. When my flu test came back negative, my medical clinic tested me for COVID-19. Seven days later at nine o'clock at night, an email arrived with a positive result. My initial worry was passing this on to Neda, my wife. Not only was she my saving grace, I didn't want her to go through this agony. Luckily, she felt fine and was probably asymptomatic.

While recovering from COVID, I relished the opportunity to work from home, as the new norm. I joined online webinars and studied with experts to get educated on this disease as fast as possible, all while checking in with my friends, corporate colleagues, and teams across the world. I became eager to launch startups to keep people and businesses safe during the pandemic. I saw opportunities for reinvention everywhere, while my self-care began to dwindle. COVID recovery demands fresh air, nourishment, and plenty of rest. Finding balance to my day became a necessity for survival, and it reinforced the main theme of this book.

My children, now in their early twenties, are both rising stars in Corporate America. When the pandemic shut down their offices, and after Neda and I had properly quarantined, my daughter, Ava, moved back in with us and set up her new home office. Having us under one roof was a welcome surprise. Working together was the icing on the cake. Watching my kids manage the pressure of their jobs has given me fuel to keep writing. They'd emerge from their offices at seven or eight o'clock at night exhausted from the day. It was a constant reminder of how easy it is to get swept up in the intensity of corporate culture. It's a series of endless demands, like being pulled by a current into deeper parts of the ocean. You don't realize how far from shore you've drifted, and it's hard to get back. You cannot relax and expect to be rescued, nor can you tread water forever. The more you deliver, the higher the expectations are of you. The more you hit your goals, the more unreachable they will become. You try to go on vacation to catch a break, but your mind never seems to leave the office. It's a given that people will burn themselves out in Corporate America—not because they want to, but because corporations offer zero balance. It's up to you to create it.

In my 40+ year career, I've had thousands of employees and mentees all over the globe. Regardless of the language, culture, gender, or age, there's ONE statement they constantly repeat when asked how they are doing: "I'm tired." This perpetual feeling of fatigue is the corporate norm and yet, I've always tried to operate differently. I jokingly asked my daughter, "Honey, you're 24 and I'm 61. Why are you more tired than me?" It's because I've always had that image of the fisherman staring back at me. I never lost sight of my need to succeed in life according to my own standards, which requires healthy doses of work/life balance.

COVID didn't change our work demands, rather it forced us to structure our days differently. Everyone became their own boss and was free to operate on their own terms. What you wear, how much you groom, when you eat, and where you go throughout the day became 100% our choice, however, timelines and deliverables still had to be executed. Your success no longer depends on how hard you work or who you know. It's based on your steadiness and understanding of the company culture.

That's why I wrote this book for university professors and corporate leaders to share with the next generation. Regardless of your experience, this book is designed to help clear up confusion, explain the unexplainable, and strategize for problem solving in this new corporate, COVID era. I want you to hold the reins of your future, instead of being swayed by societal standards and corporate pressures. I believe it's never been more possible to define success on your own terms. It's never been easier to create the career of your dreams. On top of that, there are culture, history, and politics tied into corporate structures. You can't figure it out as you go, like you can in college or entrepreneurship.

Because of that, my closest contacts tend to be realists, problem solvers, and critical thinkers. We know that Corporate isn't there to nurture its people. It's there to make its shareholders money and to maximize employee productivity. Knowing the truth of this environment lets you make a conscious choice about how you show up, what you should expect, and what will be expected of you. You might as well learn how to maximize your impact because Corporate life can be both lucrative and enlightening.

In the next five chapters, you'll hear stories and gain advice on how to step into Corporate with a mindset and foundation that won't deplete you. You'll learn how to honestly assess your situation, navigate the chaos, lead with logic, challenge the norms, and not lose sight of work/life balance. With this knowledge, you'll be able to make sound decisions, position yourself to be trusted, and ultimately excel without having to sacrifice your family, friends, health, and hobbies.

Because I care about preserving your energy and time, I made this book brief. In just a few hours, you'll learn what it means to apply yourself, invest in yourself, and follow your interests, rather than seek titles, promotions, and rankings. You still might grow in status and salary, but that doesn't always offer lasting satisfaction or a palpable feeling of success. There are gifts in this crisis that are yours for the taking. I am here as a confidant to help you glimpse at the possibilities.

COVID isn't my first major crisis in America. My world changed forever because of the Iranian revolution. In 1975, as civil outrage began to grow in my country of origin, my father sent my brother and me to University of Texas at Austin. It wasn't planned as a permanent move to America, but rather an opportunity for education, safety, and experience. Dad envisioned us getting degrees, returning to Iran, and heading corporations back home.

While I was earning my Bachelor's degree in Electrical Engineering and my Master's degree in Biomedical Engineering, Iran became increasingly more dangerous. Access to my family became sparse and expensive, my international scholarships became null and void, and my financial security went out the window. My innocence and naivety disappeared overnight in the face of grief, racism, and isolation.

On top of that, I was a brown-skinned, Middle Easterner in Texas. Threats to my life were commonplace. Discrimination was a given. When I was ready to join Corporate America, I vowed to never be complacent--to never expect the road to be smooth. This kept my humility and entitlement in check, and it forced me to find a viable plan at every turn of my career.

My corporate life started in 1983 at Texas Instruments in Houston, Texas. I was there for 14 years as a test engineer and manager, until I moved to Bellevue, Washington, and joined Microsoft in 1997. For nearly two decades, I held a variety of positions within Microsoft Office International and was a leader in the Microsoft Windows Divisions. My pride at Microsoft was in developing the HoloLens and establishing a proven track record for disruptive technologies. I didn't strive to climb the corporate ladder, nor did I grasp for titles and promotions. And yet, these opportunities came my way through my genuine interest to learn, observe, and ask tough questions.

When I left Microsoft in 2016, I was eager to keep exploring Augmented and Virtual Reality technologies. These topics, along with Artificial Intelligence and machine learning, have always received pushback from those concerned about humans losing jobs. Today, we need these machines to fill roles that put humans at risk. No longer can we sacrifice human lives when robots can do the task with greater speed, precision, and safety. This realization gave rise to my company, ARVR Academy, established to teach Augmented Reality and Virtual Reality technology to young talents and entrepreneurs, and to give them tools and training to implement their ideas in the business world. Today, we've pivoted to include other technologies--cyber security, fiber optics, and Big Data. We currently have 10 companies in our portfolio, doing groundbreaking work. I love being surrounded by scientists, researchers, young talents, and innovative minds.

I also spent years as a dedicated, Martial Arts student. The mentality needed to compete in this sport has served me well in Corporate and in life. I've approached each day like a meeting on the mat. That doesn't mean I was focused on winning. I was there to observe my weakness, polish my strengths, study my opponent, and learn from each encounter. *How can I improve next time? What did I do well? What can't I see for myself? What is the lesson learned here?* Martial Arts takes tremendous focus and accountability. These traits enabled me to enjoy my corporate experience and find that coveted balance.

I couldn't have survived my early years without family, mentors, teachers, friends, and Iranian community. They are the heroes of this book. They're made up of executives, Fortune 500 leaders, masters of their craft, and everyday people of all ages, races, and genders. I am merely a student relaying what they taught me--demonstrating how their philosophies were applied in my life.

People often bond through crisis, and thankfully so, because COVID has caused a situation worse than any world war. We are facing economic devastation for years to come, not to mention the threat of other viruses, loss of lives, and adjusting to new norms. Industries like restaurants, hospitality, sports, travel, and entertainment had to drastically shift their operations, while industries that dealt with virtual goods, virtual presence, and cloud-based infrastructure were positioned to soar. We've entered the era of machine driven, artificial intelligence. This offers an interesting future for everyone who's willing to innovate and explore.

COVID caused us to see how much our "in-person" work experience could have been better for everyone. Who knew we wouldn't need offices to be productive? Who knew remote work would operate this smoothly? We advanced 20 years in business in basically a month by going virtual, all while trying to stay alive and care for one another. That wouldn't have happened if the virus hadn't forced it.

In this book, we'll take a look at what we lost due to COVID--not to wallow in what's gone, but to drive home the importance of asking, "Why did we do things that way?" Unfortunately, pain is a prerequisite for change, and in Corporate America, your tolerance for discomfort will be put to the test. This gives you a chance to become masterful in facing what's hard. Many of the tedious tasks you were accustomed to are now gone. You no longer have to travel for work, sit in traffic, find parking, make sure your shirts are dry-cleaned, scrape snow off your windshield, or wait until your boss has left the office so you can finally go home.

Today, you can interview for jobs anywhere in the world without having to move. You can gain access to higher-ups in a corporate environment like never before. You can study with teachers abroad and meet colleagues in (and out of) your field. No longer are you judged by outside appearance and your presence. Today, you are judged by the quality of your virtual communication. Your online communication, your global connections, and your virtual deliverables now determine how far you can go--along with your ability to manage the intensity of this time.

I had one big revelation from having COVID--it was a profound relief that I have no regrets about my life or work. Sacrifices were made, but I didn't miss the meaningful stuff, like my kids' upbringing and celebration of their achievements. My friends, family, community, and health have never gone far away from me, despite my success and strong work ethic. This is possible for you, too.

COVID helped us to rethink the way we're living, engaging in community, and doing our day-to-day jobs. Tomorrow, or maybe in the coming years, we'll find a balance between virtual and physical, but the lesson we needed to learn was that all future aspects of life must adopt a virtual nature. We also need to find middle ground in how to deal with future viruses and pandemics. We have gone from one extreme to the other. Balance will find its way, but we must also actively seek it.

INSTEAD OF WORKING TO LIVE, WE LIVED TO WORK

The virus also revealed what humans should have learned long ago. We forgot how fragile and brief life can be. Instead of working to live, we lived to work and to feed the irrational need for more material possessions. We forgot that we're only inhabitants of Mother Earth, not her dictator. This is your chance to know better and do better. As you build the future of business, you can also join the fisherman in catching your fish of the day and in carving your own path to achieve balance, richness, and fulfillment.

CHAPTER 1

EXIT THE WELL

EXIT THE WELL

"Do what you can, with what you have, where you are."

— Teddy Roosevelt

In 1985, I was at the pinnacle of my Martial Arts practice while studying under Sifu John Wang and Grand Master Chang Dongsheng. Grand Master arrived in the United States as a highly celebrated Martial Arts Master from Taiwan. As his longtime student, I had no knowledge of his disagreement with the Taiwanese. The media had accused him of not allowing young Martial Arts talents to excel since he was a winner at every tournament, and was undefeated after more than 42 years on the mat. That upset Master Chang and propelled him to set a new challenge for himself. Upon leaving the country, he publicly declared that he could train a team from anywhere in the world to beat the Taiwanese. This challenge wasn't taken lightly by Master Chang, nor his homeland.

He chose the U.S. to find students worthy of his standards. Two hundred candidates later, he eventually chose 10 of us to train for a series of tournaments, North to South, in Taiwan. I had been undefeated in my weight class and became very close with Master Chang. We traveled to Taipei with our Sifu, John S. Wang, to compete and study Shuai Chiao Martial Arts. I'd never seen so many different Kung Fu schools, teachers, and techniques. It was an unforgettable trip on multiple levels.

The Martial Arts mentality of concentration, mind over matter, and extreme discipline permeated the Chinese culture. And this competition with the U.S. was a huge deal to them. They actually made banners of us, the American competitors and Master Chang's "chosen few." Imagine going to another country to find your face splattered on billboards.

Our team did an exceptional job--claiming victory in several tournaments throughout the region, yet in a crucial match, I was defeated by a person much smaller and younger than me. At the time, I was in my mid-20s, while my opponent, Charles, age 19, was the youngest Martial Arts superstar in Taiwan. My loss was followed by my teammates' losses, which handed the national title to the team of Taiwan. This was demoralizing for me and a major defeat for Master Chang, I learned soon afterwards.

That evening, I sat with my teacher over beers to lament the devastating turn of events. I was fixated on how much work we had done and felt utterly disappointed. He said, "Listen, Michael, in the U.S., Martial Arts is just a sport for you--a couple hours, a few days per week. You carve out time for practice and competition, then you remove your uniform, take your shower, and go back to normal life. It's exercise for you. It might even be your passion, yet in Taiwan, it's a way of life. Martial Arts was born in this region."

At that moment, I recalled the Chinese reporters at our Dojo months before the tournament. They interviewed each member of our team about our training techniques. They even created and published the video footage, which the other team had watched. The preparation they had placed on ensuring victory was surprisingly extensive. And they were not secretive about it. We, on the American team, did not prepare to that extent.

My teacher said about Charles, "Have you ever seen him without that uniform? He wakes up in that uniform. He goes out to the community in that uniform, attends school in that uniform. He goes to work in it. Everything here is set up to support this discipline." He told me to recognize the cultural difference and be proud that I had made it this far.

To further enlighten, he said, "Your experience of Martial Arts in the U.S. is like a frog at the bottom of the well. You look up to see only a small portion of the sky, a tiny opening, and you think the world is that big. Coming to Taiwan has allowed you to come out of the well. Now you can see the Martial Arts world all around you." His feedback provided exactly what I needed to hear. It helped me to reframe the experience as a success in my mind. We don't know how limited our view truly is, until we're exposed to a wider vision. That made sense to me as a student and as a young professional in Corporate.

As my career progressed, I noticed how the average U.S. worker was operating from *inside* of the well. They showed up each week with low enthusiasm, while sipping their Starbucks and awaiting their next instruction. They would count down until the weekend arrived, then pick up their paycheck and perform the same routine for the next 40-plus years, until retirement. I recognized right away that Corporate America wouldn't stand for that laissez faire attitude. Corporate expects you to know what's happening around you. You cannot have tunnel vision with your tasks. You have to know how your work affects the whole operation. You must step out of the well.

This 360-degree view in Corporate gives you access to multiple facets of marketing, research, communication, and technology. There are areas of growth all around you. Like Charles who ate, slept, and breathed in his uniform, Corporate life can be demanding and all encompassing, however, when you adopt a Martial Arts mentality you can minimize the inevitable turbulence along the way.

With that said, please understand--when you enter the Corporate scene, no matter what age, it's okay to feel paranoid. You must be on your toes and on your utmost behavior. You always have to be willing to learn. You also need to take care of yourself. That's why I've dedicated this chapter to taking an honest look at what it means to work *outside* of the well, particularly now that COVID is here and we've entered a virtual landscape. COVID catapulted us into foreign terrain. You'll need to adjust to the elements, so let's begin by describing the Corporate air in which we now breathe.

PROFIT IS THE GOAL

Corporate America functions in a capitalistic system, which has one goal—to make money. Corporate is there for profit only. No other reason. Responsibility is to the shareholders, not employees. When you bring revenue to the company, that's good. There's a better return for shareholders. If you do something wrong, you reverse momentum and will likely be punished. Productivity is rewarded. Anything short of that is a problem.

While at dinner with a few execs from Amazon, Boeing, and Microsoft, our discussion moved to the cold nature of Corporate America. I told them my philosophy on the culture: "Corporate America has no mother or father. It's a bastard child." They laughed and agreed. Admittedly, I was hoping to spark debate with these powerful, corporate leaders, some I'd known throughout my career, but they could find no objections.

"If you do something amazing at work, you are put on a pedestal. You are showered with admiration. A few days later, you goof up, do something wrong? You will be shamed and erased. You might say, 'But I did that amazing thing just two days ago,' and Corporate will say, 'Yes, and we paid you for that. What are you bringing me today?' There are no entitlement or participation trophies in Corporate, and there's a lot working against you--deadlines, deliverables, staying within budget, and endless pressure to perform. You have no choice but to wake up and grow up. The sooner you know that, the better. Accepting this is step one."

YOU HAVE NO CHOICE BUT TO WAKE UP AND GROW UP.

This realization, I explained to my friends, allowed me to manage my expectations as a young professional, and it stuck with me for decades. As a Martial Arts student, the pressures of corporate life didn't seem that harsh or unfair to me, especially when I was able to implement a Martial Arts mentality. I had to "exit the well" to assess the playing field in front of me. This one action alone gave me 360-degree insight.

I continued with greater specificity, "You might be perceived as a go-getter, a leader, or a person who rarely fails. And everybody goes, 'Wow, very impressive.' One day, you screw up, come up short, or disappoint, because we're all human. Maybe something happened with your family or a friend, and it affects you horribly, but you come to work anyway, and it eventually percolates into an error. Soon everybody knows about your failure and thrives on it. People who admired you, deep inside, were likely envious of your accomplishments. To realize this is happening around you can be jarring." My executive friends continued to nod.

"Then, employees gather for a coffee break and the word starts to spread. 'Oh, my God, have you heard about John's divorce?' or 'I heard his kid did something bad,' or 'He's having health issues that are affecting his work.' All of a sudden, your allies become your enemy. Your achievements go down the drain, and that stellar perception starts to diminish."

I asked the execs, "Wouldn't it be helpful for people to know these emotional tests of tolerance and humility will happen daily?" They vehemently agreed and wanted this message to be shared. Just like Charles watching videos of my performance to ensure the title victory, Corporate professionals must accept the truth of what they'll be facing in order to prepare for battle. You have to have thick skin and plenty of resilience, which comes, in part, from knowing the pain points ahead.

You might think it's time for Corporate to change, but that's not what we are here to discuss. My goal is to help you understand why Corporate behaves this way--why *people* behave this way. Competitive, money-driven environments breed this dysfunction. Your time is better spent navigating it, rather than demanding its evolution in order for you to succeed.

When you join Corporate America, you sync up with a fast-paced and demanding culture. Accept that your limits will get pushed, along with your buttons. It's not personal. It's just humans being humans. Decisions will appear to lack logic. You'll be disappointed and defeated. You'll make mistakes and have to accept your defeated status. There's no other choice than to just keep reaching. That's what a Martial Arts student would have to do. That's how breakthroughs are reached.

Admittedly, Corporate culture can be anger inducing. One coworker, Sarah, who I worked with at Texas Instruments, had become a mentor and close colleague. I remember her getting laid off unexpectedly. Afterwards, I found out that she was supporting a family of six when her husband passed away a few years earlier. She was the hardest working engineer in our group with many years of experience under her wings. I was puzzled by her departure and questioned Corporate's decision and reasoning for such an action. There appeared to be no logic behind it. That happened 38 years ago, and it still saddens and amazes me today. Like I said before, Corporate is a bastard child with no mother or father. You cannot expect to get nurtured in this environment.

Okay, now you might be thinking, "Why would I choose to work in an environment like this?"

> CORPORATE GIVES YOU A CHANCE TO BECOME AN EXCEPTIONAL VERSION OF YOURSELF, MENTALLY SHARP, EMOTIONALLY BALANCED, AND ALWAYS EVOLVING.

Easy answer—Corporate gives you a chance to become an exceptional version of yourself, mentally sharp, emotionally balanced, and always evolving. In order to succeed, you'll have to learn how to steady yourself in the face of crisis and rely on common sense and logic, instead of opinions. You'll have no choice but to face conflict, instead of running from it, and you'll learn how to question the norm, instead of accepting it as reality. Most importantly, Corporate life is an everyday practice of facing your ego and learning to shed it. These are Martial Arts basics and the rewards of having exited the well.

In Corporate, you also get to meet talented people, build global networks, fine-tune your communication, contribute to advancements, and be at the forefront of technology. Your earnings will allow you to have the financial means to create the life of your choice. This doesn't come easy though. In the spirit of full disclosure, let's continue.

EXCRUCIATING HOURS

I remember as a young engineer at Texas Instruments in the early 1980s, I was assigned to a training in our subsidiary in Japan. It became a memorable experience. Along with my Martial Arts training, that environment gave me the discipline that I enjoy today. It also prepared me for the pressures of Corporate America.

When I arrived in Japan, a lead engineer assigned me to a team, and on the first day at work, I started packing up my things at 5 PM to head out the door, as is customary in the U.S., but nobody moved from their desks. They all continued working through 6 PM, then 7 PM and 8 PM. Hungry and jet-lagged, I asked the team leader, Masatoshi, "What time do you usually go home?" He rolled his chair outside of the office and looked towards the end of the hallway. He replied, "Not yet," and I quietly wondered why we were all waiting.

Around 9:30 PM, everyone stood up from their desks at once and left the office. I arrived back at my hotel completely exhausted. The next day, I was sure to inquire about the work hours and office routine. Masatoshi said, "No one goes home until the manager leaves." That explained why he and the others were looking at the end of the hallway every few minutes. He said that he'd lose face if he left the office before the boss.

This scenario plays out in Corporate America as well. Before COVID, my presence in the office as a manager would create a natural discipline for others. I was never a hands-on leader. I left my team alone to do their work, but when I'd arrive around 7 AM and be the last to leave around 7-8 PM, that would send a signal--while Michael is at work, everybody else should be there, too. Again, it wasn't a rule set in stone, but rather unspoken.

VIRTUAL IS THE NEW PHYSICAL

Now with the virus, you can work at your own pace and conduct a meeting from your bed. Heck, you don't even have to shave or brush your teeth. You can be late and blame it on "COVID time," and people will understand. The sudden move to employee independence has been full of wins across the board. We're seeing greater innovation, communication, efficiency, kindness, and creativity. It's like we've collectively "emerged from the well," into a new world of remote interaction.

Let's say 20-30% of employees now want to work from home. Companies are going to be fine with them doing it permanently. That's because profits are soaring during this COVID time. Working remotely seemed too risky before. The inherent lack of trust between boss and employee made these control measures a necessity. Office hours and vacation time were implemented to ensure productivity. Plus, there was office space to be occupied. Why not keep an eye on everyone to minimize failure of delivery? That didn't prove to be as effective as we thought, and it wasn't cost effective either.

Workforces have been trained to be robots. Management wanted to be able to look at people and tell them what to do. Their meetings had to be in-person, and if you dozed off, it was not good. If you didn't sit up straight, that sent a signal too. A person's physical style of interacting could influence their company trajectory. Body language, dress, and grooming all played a role in your growth in corporate. All of that is diminished now. There's no physical layer.

In a few short weeks, Corporate realized that by putting employees inside a physical box, they may have been preventing them from thinking *outside* of the box. Perhaps office space and office hours were more restrictive than they realized? Lucky for you, it's a new era where you're no longer being boxed into anything, however, your follow-through and deliverables still matter more than ever. To get it all done properly, you'll need to have the focus and discipline of a Martial Arts student. You'll need to "exit the well" and understand all the moving pieces and partners associated with your project.

IN A FEW SHORT WEEKS, CORPORATE REALIZED THAT BY PUTTING EMPLOYEES INSIDE A PHYSICAL BOX, THEY MAY HAVE BEEN PREVENTING THEM FROM THINKING *OUTSIDE* OF THE BOX.

About 10-12 years ago, one of our top developers in the Bellevue headquarters of Microsoft asked if he could work remotely from his hometown in Canada. He was a newly-wed whose wife longed to be near their families again. This was a big request that needed VP approval. Before COVID, requests to work remotely were not encouraged. It would single you out and limit your growth and performance in the company. We didn't have much of a success model to follow, so the decision was complex. Because this guy had a stellar track record of productivity and expertise, he was granted permission to make the move.

I remember feeling so proud of him. He wound up working even harder. I knew more about what he was doing in Canada than when he was in the Redmond office. He'd inform us, "I'm taking my kids to the doctor at 10:45 AM. I'll be back at noon and will make up for the lost time." His deliverables went through the roof because he was disciplined, and because we gave him what he wanted. He was actually one of the few employees who were promoted while working from home. It was a glimpse into how remote work can be good for all. Looking back, we should have been suggesting it more as an option for employees. We clearly were not ready to challenge the norm of office culture. Like the frog at the bottom of the well, our vision was still limited, but not for long.

When COVID ramped up, corporations told their teams to start setting up in their homes, apartments, and studios. This transition took only one week--*one week!* No one imagined it would be as smooth as it turned out to be. That doesn't negate anyone's fears of getting sick or the obvious inconveniences, but from a 'bottom line" perspective, the office-to-home migration has been very positive for companies.

When Microsoft, Amazon, and Google told their people to work from home as long as they would like, there was a collective sigh of relief. Employees were like, "Holy shit, I'm in heaven! No traffic, no business attire, no one's watching me. My family can be safe." And the private sector was like, "Holy shit. We're in heaven! No lawsuits, no illnesses, no extensive cleaning, and our employees are still working hard." This gave Corporate time to figure out their next moves. Initially, corporations wondered if they'd have to rent bigger spaces to fit employees at six-feet social distance. They also wondered how to keep the elevators, staircases, desks, kitchens, meeting rooms, doorknobs, and bathrooms properly sanitized at all times. The list of demands was endless.

Now that there's tangible proof (and not a theory) that workers can be trusted to work remotely, why not ditch the building or downsize? Corporate America is weighing this decision from a safety and cost perspective. It's easy to do the math and see the vast savings. Let's say a midsize company pays $50,000 per year for their offices, plus $5,000 each for a handful of parking spots, a few thousand for coffee, pastries, and the occasional employee meal. Right away, that's a savings of $100,000. We didn't even mention utility costs. The writing is on the wall--buildings will be viewed by many as an unnecessary expense, at least for midsize companies. To unload an expense that large is a chance to "step out of the well" and entertain a vast array of options.

There's one big concern I have about everyone working from home--exposure to germs in public is what strengthens our immunity. As we limit contact to defend against germs and viruses attacking the body, at the same time, we are lowering our body's immune system. What's going to happen when we go back in public? These unknowns make it hard to determine the proper course of action for businesses. Industries are being forced to change, as our immune response becomes more compromised.

Restaurants, for instance, had always strived for maximum occupancy. In swanky New York City and Las Vegas restaurants, customers simply had to endure while the people at the next table were practically breathing on them. There was no privacy or personal space, but we didn't push back. We accepted the discomfort because the restaurant was rated high in reviews. We didn't want to miss the hype!

Now we're saying, "There's no way I'm going back to that place." Well, it won't open anyway, unless there's adequate social distance, high-level sanitation, and servers/chefs wearing masks. Pre-COVID, these safety measures would have seemed extreme, yet we will not allow ourselves to get packed like sardines any longer. Change was overdue and needed to happen somehow. Today, if a restaurant employee comes to work with COVID, it could create a domino effect of death for everyone who works and eats there. These concerns affect Corporate today as well. Most office layouts do not fit current guidelines for safety.

I've also been thinking about how we blindly trusted restaurants with our health. You rarely hear someone say they caught a cold or the flu "at a restaurant." When we get sick, we tend to blame the people close to us. But what about that guy who sneezed within inches of you at lunch? What about the server who was inches away when taking your order? Had we been giving adequate thought to *their* health or sanitation? These are now common and legitimate concerns, as we try to enjoy the new norm and stay safe.

In this first year of COVID, sports and entertainment industries have been pushing to open their communities, but having to cancel games, shows, or the whole season. They're not alone. Unless the airline industry comes up with a robust solution to safety, they're going to keep struggling, too. Same with hospitality, restaurants, commercial buildings, public transportation, malls, department stores, and cruise ships. They will not go away completely, but a big metamorphosis is underway. I point to these industries because Corporate intersects with all of them. As industries adjust to new regulations, Corporate transitions will continue to take place.

Recent changes are both cleansing and overdue, not just in business procedures and the switch to virtual work, but also in management. Mid-level management has always been the liaison between the workers and higher levels. Their core purpose was to be a physical buffer and to provide a ladder into leadership. But now with virtual workspaces, top-tier management no longer requires the same boundaries. That puts middle management's usefulness into question.

When people quit their jobs, it's often because of a boss they didn't like. It's often said, "People leave their boss, not the company." If we can eliminate this common source of turnover, both employee satisfaction and profits could increase. If employees keep demonstrating and demanding independence, the costs of middle management will most definitely be scrutinized. This is a big change we are seeing in the Corporate hierarchy.

YOU'RE NOW THE BOSS

We've all become used to getting up, getting dressed, and getting into the office. But when you wake up now, you're not going anywhere. You just log in and attend to your daily routines. In between, you can exercise, watch a movie, prepare meals, or put off work until evening. Nobody's watching you. Don't view this as a temporary change. Depending on your company and position, you might never have to work at an office again.

Facebook CEO Mark Zuckerberg recently predicted that 50% of his company's employees could be working remotely within the next five to 10 years.[1] That opens a huge opportunity for everybody to think global. You can be in Kalamazoo, Michigan, and get a job in Quebec, Berlin, or Dublin, and vice versa.

CNBC reported, "Zuckerberg announced that Facebook is going to "aggressively" ramp up its hiring of remote workers, and the company is going to take a "measured approach" to opening up permanent remote work positions for existing employees. Zuckerberg made his prediction on his weekly livestream with employees, telling them that this decision should help the company improve its employee retention, and it will allow Facebook to hire from talent pools that previously wouldn't consider moving to big cities to work for the company. Additionally, this decision will allow Facebook to improve the diversity of its workforce and spread economic opportunity across more places."[2]

Facebook isn't the only one following this work-from-home trend. Industries that deal with virtual goods, virtual presence, and cloud-based infrastructure are freeing themselves from needing both office space and employees. We have entered the era of machine driven, artificial intelligence, which doesn't necessarily mean opportunities will go away for workers. For years, Amazon has been investing heavily in robotics at their fulfillment centers to keep up with their demand. During the pandemic, these revolutionary machines did not diminish jobs. Amazon actually added 248,500 new workers to address these robotic needs.[3] Isn't it fascinating that additional people were needed to ensure technology was running smoothly? It feels as though we have "exited the well" and are engaging more with robotics and less with humans.

THE VIRTUAL LEARNING CURVE

Let's be honest, the virtual world has plenty of technical challenges. We have to deal with cameras, internet, audio/video, connectivity, and bandwidth, to name a few. We took for granted that all of this was provided back at the office. Now, we have to troubleshoot on a constant basis and fix paper jams in the printer. I just heard the CEO of a major Seattle hospital say that the technology challenges in his home are much harder than performing neurosurgery these days.

It makes me laugh to remember when email management was the biggest of our hassles. You had to be careful not to insult anyone or use insensitive words. You had to keep up with the volume of responses in your inbox. Now, you have to think about your video presence. In virtual meetings, it's easy to hit the record button. You never know who's recording what. Not only are your words documented, so are your appearance and facial expressions.

This means you cannot get too casual in meetings. I have seen plenty of bloopers and "real life" incidents in the last few months--colleagues falling asleep, dogs barking, kids crying, and half-clothed family members. Make sure your background is filtered on video, and whatever your screen shows, have it reflect your professionalism. A simple error can live in the cloud forever.

The essence of surviving in a company still hasn't changed. You still need to behave, have discipline, form connections, be resilient, and most of all, you still need to deliver. Your only limitation, as my son puts it, is "me vs. me." It might seem like Corporate presents a variety of obstacles, but they are far less obtrusive, if you stay vigilant in examining your habits and accepting the truth of the Corporate scene. This is what separates Corporate leaders from Corporate employees--the drive to continuously improve and the desire to keep forging ahead.

As a leader, entrepreneur, innovator, scientist, or anybody who wants to excel in life, you've been given a chance to refine and reinvent yourself in this new, virtual era. The average worker stays inside of the well, unaware of their limited view. Yet when you work in Corporate America, you have no choice but to "exit the well" and submerge yourself in the fast-paced intensity of capitalism.

Like a Martial Arts student, you have to become quick, smart, and aware. You now also have to live in a culture with multiple viruses. That's why virtual has become the new physical. You've been catapulted into an era of safety, machines, less human contact, and the chance to be your own boss. The choice is yours--do you want to lean on your elbow during Martial Arts class, or do you want to bow on the mat, as a master of adaptability?

In the next few chapters, we'll dig deeper into the inevitable emotions you might feel in Corporate. It's one thing to adjust our lives in this COVID era, it's another to stay focused when our country is politically charged and increasingly divided. My immigrant experiences haven't been easy, but they've taught me how to navigate through revolutionary times. If you can relate to being different from dominant culture; maybe you're LGBTQ, a person of color, or you manage ADHD, mental health, trauma, or a physical disability, I hope my stories demonstrate how adversity doesn't have to limit you.

CHAPTER 2

FIND THE GIFTS OF CRISIS

FIND THE GIFTS
OF CRISIS

"Pain is inevitable, suffering is optional."

— Haruki Murakami

Do you remember when phone books were the primary source of finding each other? This essential compilation of names and addresses would utterly fascinate me. I would sit in phone booths and peruse the phone book for hours. People always chuckle when I confess to having this peculiar hobby. It certainly signifies my love for copious data. While phone book memories offer a pleasant whiff of nostalgia, they've also been used as a tool to threaten my life.

Early November 1979, there was a knock at the door. Back then, you never asked who was there before grabbing the doorknob. You trusted it was a neighbor or friend. At the time, I was living alone and working on my Bachelor of Electrical Engineering at University of Texas at Austin. After putting dinner in the oven, I swung open the door to find four, angry-looking guys with beers in hand.

They said, "If you hurt the hostages in Iran, we're going to kill you."

A little background: The Iranian Revolution and the over-throw of the Pahlavi Dynasty led to extreme tension be-tween the U.S. and the newly installed, Islamic Republic government. Following these events on November 4, 1979, a group of Muslim students took over the U.S. embassy in

Tehran and held 52 American diplomats and citizens hostage for 444 days.

To detour my unwelcome guests, I pretended to be distracted by people in another room. I turned my head and shouted to a (fake) group of friends, "Hey guys, I'll be with you momentarily." Scared for my life, I had to think fast and keep my cool. "Sorry, I have a bunch of friends here," I told them. "What were you saying?"

They repeated, "If you hurt the hostages in Iran, we're going to kill you." "What hostages?" I asked, sincerely confused. Keep in mind, this was pre-internet, when media coverage wasn't as dominant. There might be a snippet of news from Iran, mostly saying that tensions were high.

My next move was to ask how they knew me. Apparently, these guys had been playing the "weird name" phone book game–luck of the draw, Nassirian appeared, along with my home address. This gave them a way to retaliate for the hostage crisis in Iran. Thankfully, I didn't get hurt. They wound up screaming obscenities for about a minute, then walking away. Claiming to have guests in the next room might have saved my life that day. I'll never know.

Texas was terrifying for the Iranian community in the 80s. One of my friends was shot point-blank at a bar. After we finished studying in the library, he went out alone for a beer. When he didn't show up the next day for the test, it took two weeks before we could identify him in the morgue. The officer just sat there chewing tobacco and spitting in a cup. "I reckon it was a crime of passion," he told us. That was his lame justification for my friend's sudden death.

Iranians in the U.S. have encountered beatings, chasings, insults, and hold-ups at knife and gunpoint. The hate for us was always looming, and campus police did nothing to ensure safety. We had to build a schedule for women, children, and the elderly to get where they needed to go harm-free. My innocent view of the world disappeared during this time, which didn't make me turn against humankind. It actually grew my capacity to care for myself and others. It also pushed me to find mentors and to see the surprising gifts that can arise in crisis.

The purpose of this chapter is to acknowledge that none of us are immune to personal or professional crises. We will have accidents, illnesses, chaos, mistakes, betrayals, disappointments, and deaths, yet in the cracks of despair, gifts and lessons will eventually present themselves. One natural consequence of a crisis is the strengthening of bonds with friends, family, coworkers, and community. When times get tough, people pull together in surprising ways.

WITH ONLY A QUARTER

Before the hostage crisis, my brother and I had been fully funded by our parents. I remember us as being "fat, dumb, and happy" with our expenses paid--car, apartments, food, and schooling. As international students with scholarships, we had only anticipated hard work at school, not so much in life. Yet as tension continued to rise in Iran, my parents became more difficult and expensive to reach. Our scholarships froze, as did my parents' access to sending money. With limited family, safety, and funds, my world became very small. During holidays, when everyone went home to their families, I'd be stuck on campus alone with no aunts or uncles to invite me over.

I wouldn't have survived my college days if not for the help of two professors. I remember going back to my apartment after paying tuition and rent. My only remaining money was a single quarter in my pocket. I sat awake all night wondering what was next for me. *How will I pay for school going forward? How will I afford rent? How will I buy books for the semester? How will I eat?*

The answer was clear—get a job immediately. But hadn't ever worked a day in my life. The next morning, I hopped on my bike at 6 AM and sat in front of the Engineering and Science Building at University of Texas. I kept thinking, "What can I do?" while pleading with God. "If you help me get out of the situation, I promise to give it back."

One of my advisors, Professor Dr. John Cogdell, walked by and asked what I was doing there so early. I told him how badly I needed a job at the department. He said, "Wait here. I have to do my daily run." He put on his shorts, went for a jog, and came back around 7:15 AM. (I have such vivid recollections of this day.)

When he walked in the door, I attached myself to him everywhere he went. He noticed me again. "So what is it?" I told him I desperately needed a job. "Too late. All jobs have been allocated." "But I don't have any money," I confessed. He told me to hold on because he had to take a shower. I stood outside of the shower waiting on Dr. Cogdell, while my prayers and anxieties continued.

Finally, he invited me into his office. "Do you know Dr. Ian Thomas?" Yes, I had been a student in his class. He said, "Dr. Thomas may have 17 hours, but you need 20 hours to be eligible to get an in-state tuition. Go talk to him." He gave me Dr. Thomas's number, and with that one remaining quarter in my pocket, I sat next to the phone booth on my bike and waited for a decent hour in the morning to make the call. By now, my panic in losing this opportunity was at an all-time high. It felt like my only option.

Around 9 AM, I dialed his number with nervous anticipation. "Hello, Dr. Thomas?" My voice was trembling, and I didn't know what to say. "This is Michael Nassirian." He quickly replied, "Michael, of course, how are you? How's your family?" I couldn't believe he knew me! "Of course, I know you," he said. "You aced all of my tests. In a class of 600, you really shined." In this dire moment of seeking security, I didn't even notice he was complimenting me.

He asked again, "How's your mom and dad? I've been reading about the revolution in Iran." Since Dr. Thomas was from Australia, he followed world news. "What can I do for you?" he asked. I explained that I need a job, and Dr Cogdell had sent me. "Where are you right now, Michael?" "In front of the Engineering and Science Building." He told me not to move. A half an hour later, his yellow Volkswagen bug drove into the parking lot for a meeting with Dr. Cogdell and me.

Dr. Cogdell explained the situation--there were only 17 hours left in Dr. Thomas's budget. I needed 20. With zero hesitation, Dr. Thomas replied, "Give them to Mike. I'm done interviewing." "But you'll have to find three more hours to make him eligible for in-state tuition." Dr. Thomas quipped back, "Take it out of my own budget."

I sat there in complete shock and relief. Dr. Thomas was my savior that day. He even took me to his house afterwards to make me a sandwich because I hadn't eaten in two days. His actions demonstrated how much impact we can have on each other, and how one kind gesture can change someone's entire life. Because Dr. Thomas and Dr. Cogdell made their time and resources available to me, I now offer the same to anyone who wants to contact me for coaching, brainstorming, or advice. If I can be someone's Dr. Thomas, what a mutual blessing that could be.

Later, Dr. Cogdell mentioned that Dr. Thomas had interviewed at least 15 students for the job. "Whatever you did," he whispered, "keep on doing it." For the first time, I grasped how beneficial my hard work and attention to detail had actually been. Besides securing that job, Dr. Cogdell's feedback about my efforts was one of those gifts of crisis. When you give your all, the rewards might not appear immediately, but rather when you least expect them.

During this time, I also learned that crisis takes many forms, and that complacency would no longer be an option for me. This was an opportunity to become more responsive, vigilant, and grateful for what I had in my life. In the 80s when Saddam Hussein was attacking Iran, I lived through nearly 24 hours of believing my family had been bombed to death. On a call with my dad, he sounded distressed. "I cannot find your mom or sister. They left the house earlier, and I don't know where they are." All of a sudden, a gigantic explosion came over the phone, followed by disconnection.

What was I expected to think? I sat on the ground crying-fully convinced that I'd just lost my family. I went back to work and told my manager, "I'm going back to Iran." He dropped everything to hear me explain what had occurred. As my brother and I rushed to find our passports, the phone rang. Dad exclaimed, "I found your mom and sister! The explosion was close, but didn't hit our house." Luckily, I did not lose my parents that day, but that experience reinforced that life is precious and complacency is unacceptable.

Perhaps you might have lost a loved one to COVID, or your industry was destroyed, or your position was dissolved when everyone started remote working. Having an easy life isn't guaranteed to anyone. Crisis has a way of reminding us to savor the good moments and find good people who can offer help.

KINDNESS ON THE RISE

In this time of COVID, we're more encouraged than ever to hear people's feelings and struggles, and to address oppression in its various forms. That's what excites me about the residual effects of this virus. *Might we treat each other better? Might we be kinder to Mother Earth? Might we find more happiness at work?*

We are seeing a rise in social ethics, which is yet another gift of crisis. During the lockdown, people reached out to friends and family with messages of love. We checked in on the elderly and donated to the disadvantaged. We hosted special events on Zoom and drove by people's homes flashing "Happy Birthday" signs. Then, the Black Lives Matter movement exploded after the killing of George Floyd. These events remind us that we need to take better care of each other. If not now, when?

Corporate America heard the message loud and clear, and is taking steps to make employees a priority. You might be thinking, "Wait, didn't you just say capitalism is focused on profit?" Yes, that's still true. If employees feel safe working for a company, it will have a positive impact on revenue. If there's trust between company and worker, it will offer greater stability. That's why corporations have adopted diversity, equity, and inclusion (DEI) training. It was time to face the facts and listen to people's voices--not just for the people, but for the company's safety and evolution, too.

Today, employees are considered the essence of the workforce. Your preferences and pronouns are being given increasing consideration. This transformation has taken decades and is still underway. It's become a call for leadership to step up and notice not only the marginalized team members around them, but also anyone who's in need. This responsibility for inclusion rests with management.

CROSS-GENERATIONAL CONNECTION

When I was a manager, I deemed every third Tuesday "Lunch with Michael." Each person on my team had their designated month when lunch would be my treat. There was only one rule--no discussions about work. This was a chance to learn about our lives outside of work--hobbies, families, projects, music, traveling, etc. During these lunches, I would sit there absorbed in the stories of Jason's vegetable garden, Tony's new dog, or Susan's ultra-marathon. This was relaxing, and I'd share parts of my life with them too. It helped us to understand each other more, so when crisis or difficulty would arise, I'd be better equipped at addressing their needs.

Lunches with your staff might not be an option at this time, but you need to initiate virtual connection with your people somehow. You could always have an impressive lunch (employee's choice) delivered to their residence. Then, you can join them online for a meal and a chat about what's happening in their lives. Birthdays, happy hours, work anniversaries, and congratulations should be celebrated on a regular basis--just as struggles, mistakes, grief, and disappointment need to be acknowledged as well. This is the environment Corporate must now create online. The COVID crisis forced us to be more creative and intentional in how we connect.

As I write this in May 2020, it's the third month of COVID quarantine. Most businesses in Bellevue, Washington are still limited or shut down completely. Cases of the virus keep increasing, and people are still tucked away in their homes. My family and I are running several businesses from our home. My wife has a translation company, I have several startups, plus we have two young professionals who work in corporations.

It's been one of the most interesting and rewarding experiences to have my kids under the same roof, while we all work. I love when they come to me for help with tasks and concerns, but they mostly want advice on what to say or do in certain situations. Sometimes they need to vent about the manager who did this, or the coworker who did that, or the customer who said this thing. I listen, but not for too long because they usually only need a few common-sense pointers before heading back to work. The same is true for my students and mentees. I've been blown away by the younger generation's ability to quickly adapt and take things in stride.

My daughter Ava is a perfect example of younger generation resilience. In mid-March, she moved from Washington, DC because Amazon had closed all their offices. She had only moved there months before and was just getting settled. Now, she's back in our Bellevue home. Every morning, sometimes as early as 5 AM, she is sitting at her makeshift office, doing her job, as if nothing had changed. She works out, makes lunch, and is impressive in her management of time.

By 5-6 PM on Fridays, my kids start their social interactions online--COVID style. My daughter yelled out to me, "Dad, come here and meet my team!" As I scanned the screen, I saw about 10 people from Chicago, California, Texas, and Seattle. Everyone was laughing and blowing off steam from the week. My son Baabak had a social hour with his buddies the other day via Zoom. He's continued to "see" his friends with minimal disruption. These kids are re-inventing a new norm where physical location is not always needed. They demonstrate how crises can grow your resilience and teach you to gather friends in new ways.

Older generations have slowed down advancements because of their need to have coffee, shake hands, and do things traditionally. This is no longer a luxury we can afford. Those who have long-standing, ingrained habits are struggling mightily during this time. We need to be flexible. I told my friends, "Okay, this Friday, we're going to have virtual poker." We did, and it was better than we thought. We are learning new ways to work, live, and socialize. Younger generations are reminding us to drop rigidity. We have to limber up sometimes.

I must also give credit to the elders of the business community. People my age are always helping young ones in their industry. Many fund entrepreneurs and mentor corporate executives. Many of them donate to make communities better. Many of them have survived their own private nightmares, so their insights carry significant weight at this time. Having multi-generational wisdom is helpful in life, particularly when a crisis occurs and the gifts seem impossible to find.

I've needed my mentors most when I've screwed up and had to figure out my next steps. When addressing them for help, I would always state my problem or discomfort, and then let them share their advice or pertinent story. Over time, I learned to be quiet and not to interrupt. God gave us two ears and one mouth. We should listen twice as much as we talk. Regardless of whether I applied their advice or not, these interactions grew my networks and pushed me to innovate in business and in life.

FIND YOUR MENTORS

Mentorships in companies can be fruitful. They can also feel forced. Not everyone likes to be transparent about their struggles. Not everyone wants to dedicate time to helping others, but if the mentor starts as a friend or an "unofficial mentor," those are sometimes the best ones to have. They don't have to be high level vice presidents. They don't have to be super visible. Just make sure they are out of your department, and remember to honor their time and wisdom.

Kevin Turner was the COO at Microsoft for many years. In one of his managerial series, he talked about his private meetings with Jack Welch, who was pretty much the CEO of all CEOs. Jack has contributed to countless leaders' success. Sadly, he passed away, just as I was starting this book. I was eager to send him a copy and wanted to make him proud of what I'd learned from him. In any case, he gave a lesson to Kevin Turner that was powerful enough to be repeated.

In a weekly one-hour meeting, Jack told Kevin that he had three observations about what he could be doing differently. Kevin could hardly wait to hear his advice. After the first insight from Jack, Kevin said he went on a talking spree, where he felt the need to explain himself at length. After an impassioned 45-minute rant, he stopped and asked Jack for his second observation. Jack said, "No, that's good and enough for today." Kevin left the meeting knowing he had made a grave error. Jack followed up by cancelling all of Kevin's weekly and bimonthly meetings. Ouch!

Heartbroken, Kevin went to his mentor who told him that if he ever got in that office again, just shut up and take notes. "Be a sponge--absorb." Kevin eventually got another chance with Jack, and you can bet his silence led to an illuminating experience with this highly regarded leader. He learned a lesson of a lifetime--err on the side of listening, rather than explaining when you're in front of people you admire. A good mentor will hand you those hard truths, pat you on the back, and tell you to get back in the game.

None of us would willingly invite pain into our lives. We don't try to screw up. We don't seek embarrassment or shame, yet when it happens, the lessons are often quite memorable. People need to go through a harsh reality to reach next-level advancements in business and in life. If we could bypass the difficulty, that would be great, however, it appears we do our best growing, learning, and connecting when our feet are held to the fire.

NONE OF US WOULD WILLINGLY INVITE PAIN INTO OUR LIVES. WE DON'T TRY TO SCREW UP. WE DON'T SEEK EMBARRASSMENT OR SHAME, YET WHEN IT HAPPENS, THE LESSONS ARE OFTEN QUITE MEMORABLE.

In Corporate America, you can't expect anyone to come to your rescue. Crises will happen in your teams, on your projects, in the company, and in your life. Racism and discrimination aren't going to go away completely either. Moments of joy will arise, but when a crisis occurs, that's when you can truly build resilience and strengthen bonds with the people around you. Don't lose sight of the gifts that are trying to present themselves.

In the next chapter, you'll hear more stories of discrimination from my immigrant experience. My goal isn't to seek sympathy, but to demonstrate how I got to the place of not being triggered by anyone's opinion. This doesn't mean I don't care, or that I've shut down my feelings. It means that I seek places where I can be involved in creating solutions and studying facts, instead of steeping in the drama. Let me help you channel your passion in a productive fashion. You're about to discover the value of using logic and common sense as your daily compass.

CHAPTER 3

LEAD WITH LOGIC

LEAD WITH LOGIC

"Science is a willingness to accept facts even
when they are opposed to wishes."

— B.F. Skinner

There's a story I've told for years that's perfect for our current times:

> A guy was speeding through a quaint, Italian village in his Ferrari. The road was narrow, and this man was taking curves at 50 miles an hour. When he passed a biker, nearly hitting him, the biker shouted, "Pig!" Ferrari Guy shrugged it off and yelled, "Yeah, you too, buddy." As he barreled around the next turn, lo and behold—he ran straight into a gigantic herd of pigs.

Ferrari Guy wasn't being insulted, he was being given advance notice about the danger ahead. He was breaking the law and jeopardizing the safety of everyone in town. If he had fine-tuned his reflection skills, he would have slowed down and said, "Oh, maybe there's a pig in the road." The lesson? Emotions cloud facts! When you think you're being insulted, when you think you're beyond reproach, there just might be a hidden message waiting for you. To receive it, you must learn to step back, reflect, and cope with what you just heard.

At this point in the book, you've learned the importance of stepping "outside of the well." The intensity of Corporate

America will catapult you into a world where your humility and dedication are required every day. Burnout is a given. You have to define what balance means for you and pursue it as a daily habit.

We also discussed how to find the gifts in crisis. No one wants to deal with failures and catastrophes, but they allow for greater innovation, safety, and connections. Now, let's focus on using logic to lead your thoughts. I hope my stories in this chapter will add equilibrium to your everyday decisions and help you see the value in using logic and common sense, particularly when others are incapable of doing so.

Before we go any further, please answer these questions honestly:

When controversy runs high, are you able to regulate your response?

Can you withstand personal attacks on your values or perspectives?

If your boss, coworker, or client supports a politician that you can't stand, can you still find rapport with them?

Do people's beliefs and behavior derail your progress at work?

With President Trump in office, these dynamics have been increasingly problematic. Believe me, I did not want to talk about politics, inequity, and injustice in this book, nor am I an expert on these topics. But whether you like it or not, they are a primary focus of attention right now and a source of pain for many. As a result, we are divided as a country--fixated on cancel culture and the media drama of the day. This affects people's productivity at work, and it gives them tunnel vision, like the frog at the bottom of the well.

After 40 years in Corporate, my immigrant experience taught me how to have a big picture view of discrimination and politics. I truly do not get triggered by anyone. This has created an environment where people feel like they can talk to me about anything. I collect facts and data. I use logic and common sense when shaping my opinions. If you want to create an environment of transparency with others, and if you want to regulate the negative effects of politics on your own mood, then my outlook may be helpful to you.

Since the virus began, we've been hearing about increases in domestic violence, child abuse, and addiction. Mental health issues and suicide are magnified at this time as well. When people are struggling or irritated, they don't bring their best selves to work. They'll start to form cliques and make snap judgements. They follow group mentality, instead of thinking for themselves. They'll let cell phones and social media pull them away from their daily duties. Their team culture becomes toxic, their effectiveness wanes, and their communication can turn passive aggressive. None of this will fly in Corporate America. It's simply not worth risking your clout and client relations.

Here are six strategies to lead with logic and find balance in your thoughts and ideas:

1. THINK LIKE AN IMMIGRANT

In America, a high percentage of Iranians are successful. That isn't an anomaly. It has been a necessity of survival for us. American immigrant workers, on the whole, can serve as role models during this pandemic era. That's because we operate on logic with great consistency. This isn't our first political upheaval. This isn't the first time we've been isolated. We've always had to be hypervigilant. We've always been forced to examine, what's the big picture here? What else is there for me to learn? What's the smartest action for me to take?

That's why I suggest you think like an immigrant, regardless of Corporate's progress in sensitivity and equality. That means you keep your eye on the goal and not on what you wish was different. It also means you keep your cool as much as possible. It can be hard to find neutrality and common sense when you're upset. Yet the coping skills you hone for Corporate could also come in handy if there's a life or death situation.

At a Midland/Odessa facility for Texas Instruments, our team leader, Brian, invited me for a Saturday morning jog with him. He was an athletic guy and thought we'd be compatible running mates because of my Martial Arts background. I didn't have the heart to tell him that I didn't own a pair of running shoes. The night before, I made the necessary purchase and hoped for the best.

The next day, I arrived at what I thought was the destination Brian had proposed. After parking the car, I started to jog lightly in search of Brian. That's when I stumbled on a group of KKK demonstrators. Knowing they were harmful to Black people, I didn't feel an immediate threat, however, I certainly didn't feel welcome either. When I deliberately started walking in the opposite direction, they slowly began to surround me. One guy shouted, *Where you goin, boy?*

Admittedly, I was naive to the situation, not realizing the KKK cast a wider net on all foreigners. Because I thought I'd be okay, I just acted normal and explained that I was trying to catch up with a friend. When they wouldn't let me go, I still didn't panic, but rather became intrigued at why I was a target.

"You foreigners are taking our jobs," they shouted. Surprised, I said, "Oh, I'm sorry to hear that. Are you engineers? Are you involved in semiconductors? If that's the case, I apologize." A guy named Burt responded, "No, we're in manufacturing."

This kicked off a lengthy conversation between us, which continued on Burt's front porch. The group disarmed and can you believe Burt wanted to have beers with me? I sat there sipping Coors at 10 in the morning, listening to him talk about his life.

When there was a natural pause in conversation, I asked to use Burt's phone--hoping Brian would come and get me. Turns out, I had screwed up the directions he'd originally given me. When his car pulled in the driveway, Brian's eyes grew wide at the sight of white robes. Even as a white man, he refused to get out of the car. As I jumped into his front seat, we both breathed a sigh of relief. Back at work, everyone joked that "Michael has KKK friends now."

In reality, that was a life and death situation. Had I been a Black person, it would have been terrifying. Not realizing the potential for threat, indeed, helped me stay cool, but there was one thing I knew for sure--if I had used my Martial Arts techniques or a harsh tone with these guys, it wouldn't have ended well. If I told them they were stupid or had no education, it would have been dangerous. Logic is something that you cannot deviate from in life. Add common sense, and your decisions will get even better. Because I knew my ability to stay calm and listen with sincerity, I was able to access both rationality and patience.

> **LOGIC IS SOMETHING THAT YOU CANNOT DEVIATE FROM IN LIFE. ADD COMMON SENSE, AND YOUR DECISIONS WILL GET EVEN BETTER.**

2. KNOW YOUR STRENGTHS

When I was a young engineer at Texas Instruments in the military semiconductor division, my manager never called me by my name. He would call me the short shit, college boy, new kid, or that foreign guy--whatever came to his mind. I've already explained the discriminatory scene that I faced in Texas in the 80s. As a brown-skinned immigrant with an accent, I was prepared for Corporate America to be no different.

So this manager did not offend me. Employees were considered laborers back then. Our roles, timelines, and deliverables were all dictated. Our feelings were irrelevant. I was just happy to be noticed by my manager, happy to be given tasks. I'd respond, "Hi, I'm Michael!" He did not care, nor did it matter. Do you know why?

Within one year, I had advanced into another department, and within two years, I was leading a small team of engineers at the Military Semiconductor department of Texas Instruments. I knew my strengths and knew I could deliver at work. My focus was placed on that which I could control, which is mostly myself, rather than requiring outside forces to change. This has been a key element to my success and peace of mind.

Companies are setting new standards of conduct, one that is more kind, inclusive, and diverse, but people's biases and habits don't change instantaneously. Those who are not part of the dominant culture, due to race, religion, ability, sexual orientation, or gender, must find discernment strategies and even outside help to stay strong throughout their day.

One of my mentees was born in South America and is a young engineer at a large U.S. company. She recently came to me in tears, insisting that the white, blonde-haired women at her work were given easier tasks. She was certain this was a blatant act of prejudice. There was no convincing her otherwise.

As she was crying in my office, I started thinking about how she's one of the top producers in her organization, and how her manager had been raving to me about her performance. I also remembered that blonde, white women made up 80% of the team. My mentee continued, "When there's a customer no one wants to work with, these assignments are always given to me! Never to the blonde, white girls!"

After letting her vent, I explained how she'd been given a chance to impress and get promoted. "Your manager is giving you something that no one else can grasp--the challenge of serving this unique customer." So we talked about how to solve the clients' problems, which she did with patience and persistence. Shortly after, that "discriminatory" manager wound up recommending her to a newly opened division.

Her commitment to giving value back to the company got her promoted within a year--unlike the blonde, white women who were shielded from a bigger challenge and thus did not grow as my mentee had.

I tell my mentees, discrimination is going to happen, no matter what. Nothing is truly equal. Oppression is not going to disappear. Things will always be unfair and inequitable to someone. And when these situations personally affect you, there is always an opportunity to learn something new about yourself and others. Remember, this is what it means to be "outside of the well." It's not all sunny skies.

Now don't get me wrong--I'm not saying inequity should be ignored. There is always a team member or even a group who will look down on others. I have worked with managers who believed women cannot achieve. One colleague at Microsoft had about 30-40 employees under him. Female team members were continually bypassed for leadership positions. Human Resources would bring it up, yet he'd justify his actions by showing proof of male achievement.

Eventually, these women would get transferred to my group, where they would shine and quickly climb the corporate ladder. So it's not always a problem with the culture, it's the DNA of some people to look at gender, race, and sexuality with fixed and negative perceptions. Transformation can happen for some, but you owe it to yourself not to wait for others to change. Don't count on anyone to alter their political party or values system. It's not worth your energy.

3. SHIFT YOUR POLITICAL INVOLVEMENT

I learned early in life to view politics holistically. That means I don't get attached to Democrat or Republican ideology. I've seen presidents who were loved and hated—presidents with strong domestic policies and international policies, and vice versa. I've also had firsthand experience with corruption and lack of democracy, outside of U.S. borders, and I've traveled to almost every corner of the Earth.

Ford, Nixon, Reagan, Obama, Trump--I refuse to let these polarizing figures occupy my thinking or damage my relationships. I strive to collect facts and see these leaders as they truly are, so their actions don't catch me off guard. Like

President Trump whose unfiltered Twitter feed shocks people daily. I've always seen him as appealing to the construction worker in Queens, New York. Since he descended on that escalator to announce his candidacy, I've expected his words to sound the same as they did before his presidency. Why would we expect otherwise? He was elected, in part, because of his controversial style.

When you see people as they truly are, their behavior doesn't have to throw you off course. You might not like it, but you can learn to anticipate it and respond without your adrenaline skyrocketing. Then, and only then, can you view the facts about a person, place, or thing, instead of being told what to think.

For example, President Trump could have done better in managing this pandemic, yet to obsess over what he hasn't done is useless. The end result will provide ultimate proof of his competence. What happens six months or one year from now? Are we going to have 300,000 or 500,000 dead from COVID? Are we going to survive economically? Is my mortgage going to increase tenfold? How are we going to address unemployment? Are we on the verge of another

Depression? These questions are more important to me than Nancy Pelosi, Chuck Schumer, or Mitch McConnell.

This two-party system of Democrat and Republican has become limiting to us as citizens. Both parties fuel the fire, waste money, and hide truths. We give too much power and attention to these people, when in truth, there is a capitalistic system that runs the ship. I'd guess only 20% of a leader's vision winds up happening. The remaining 80% comes from the checks and balances of the oil industry, energy industry, along with imports and exports from around the world. Too often, we blame the person with a lofty title, instead of examining the system behind them.

As a country, we are struggling economically and medically. I would love to bring in highly trained experts in these areas. We, the People, should choose government leaders based on intellect, expertise, education, and specialization in the areas we desperately need to fix. We, as citizens, are of utmost importance, yet we let these two parties dictate our identities, moods, and decisions. Who gives a crap about which party you belong to when you're unemployed, under resourced, fearful of the pandemic, or battling healthcare?

Today, I see national politics has become a gigantic distraction from progress that can be made on yourself and your community. It's fine to have gripes about the government, but first ask yourself, what am I doing in my workplace, industry, or state to separate myself from that politician I can't stand? Am I part of a solution? Turn off CNN. Silence Fox News. Instead, discover what's needed in the world that's closest to you. Discontent comes from doing nothing and feeling powerless to politicians. Unsubscribe yourself from this mentality and refocus on what you can control.

President Kennedy said, "Ask not what your country can do for you. Ask what you can do for your country." When I came to this country, that mentality was basically hacked into my brain--the more I do for this country, the more I will get in return. For me, this means being vocal with our state leaders. I go to their fundraising, watch their speeches, donate to campaigns, ask questions, and write them letters. More than anything, I study what I don't understand and weigh the pros and cons of what's happening.

In your Corporate career, you'll need to exercise the same type of discernment and reasoning, not just to be happy, but to be successful. This is more important than ever because people's political frustrations often shift to intolerance. Let me assure you--there's a healthier way to focus your frustrations. Shift your political involvement to your community, and let the rest of the country fight about national politics.

4. STAY AWAY FROM ONE-SIDED OPINIONS

You should be able to tolerate opinions that are not aligned with your beliefs and understanding. That's how you improve and progress in life, yet in the last 7-8 years, there's growing intolerance for the other side. As big as the education system industry is, many universities are allowing this division to occur. What happened to listening to pros and cons and seeking feedback? Weren't we all taught to gain opposite views to strengthen our beliefs and correct our understanding? Why aren't we exercising that now? Why did it stop?

People are allowing others to define what's good, bad, right, and wrong, however, most people's views are not supported by facts. They also could be biased. Investigate for yourself. This not only holds true in politics but also corporate, community, and major decisions in life. Let your mind be open, as you absorb various views. Then do your own homework to test their legitimacy. This is how you grow your mindset. Stay away from one-sided opinions. Anyone who deems you an outcast for having independent thought is thinking in a communist mentality. It's no different than living in China.

The Chinese are not innovators, they're imitators because they require a uniform mindset--you must be successful, work hard, do what is prescribed for you. Anyone who strays is shut down and deemed an outsider. This does not allow young minds to wander or think creatively. To minimize conflict, most Chinese simply conform. Every time I visit there for business, it's clear that they're working hard. I see productivity in their factories, offices, and daily life, but when I collaborate with them, I don't see any new ideas or innovation. Is that what we want in Corporate America?

America is the land of the free. Everyone is free to express their own opinion. No one should be threatened with harm or violence for speaking their beliefs. Refusing to participate in cancel culture and mob mentality is how you can take back our country and secure your right to freedom of speech. It's also how you become safe for others to talk to because you're tolerant of a wide range of views.

5. SEEK THE WHOLE PICTURE

In 2015, the *New York Times* wrote a scathing article called "Inside Amazon: Wrestling Big Ideas in a Bruising Workplace."1 It basically said it was the worst place to work and people hated it. CEO Jeff Bezos was unapologetic in his reply. "It's not easy to work here," he told Amazon shareholders. Bezos said he didn't want to create a "country club" atmosphere, where people went to "retire."2 He was referring to Microsoft, the company across the bridge. Bezos wanted Amazon to have a perpetual start-up vibe. His point was an exercise of frugality, which he emphasizes at all his talks. He wants to separate Amazon from Corporate America's current trend of providing employees meals, hair stylists, pet grooming, car repair, and many other perks that can be found at Google, Facebook, Apple, and Microsoft.

In a friendly conversation with one of their VPs, I jokingly asked, "How's the sweatshop?" This guy is very pragmatic, and I highly respect his views. He said, "You know, it could be true. We could have areas of the company that are as bad as the article says. But the reality is, we're hiring 50,000-60,000 people a year. If attrition was as high as the article said, people would stop coming, yet they flock to get these jobs. We are also constantly improving, so I question how bad things are for long."

Facts offer balance to hype. Amazon's warehouses and fulfillment centers might need considerable attention, but Amazon has been a huge supplier of jobs. Plus, other departments are quite content. Both my kids work there and are invigorated in their positions. So you have to look at things from a holistic view, rather than just one angle.

This applies to job hunting as well. You must research a company before you interview for any position. Holistic job hunting does not mean you ignore abusive or criminal behavior. You don't want to work for Lehman Brothers and wake up in the morning to see your manager being handcuffed away from their Manhattan penthouse. At the same time, you don't want to work somewhere that's going to make you hate yourself every morning.

No place is perfect. You must decide what's going to work best for you. Give yourself this consideration. Interview as many people as you can. Learn the history of the company. Has discrimination been a problem? How does conflict get handled internally? What's the future direction of this company? What's their balance book showing? What's their perception in the industry?

I spoke recently with one of my mentees, a young woman who had just started her Corporate career. She was one of several kids who I helped transition from college to Corporate. When I asked how she's been doing, she thanked me profusely for encouraging her to question and research the prospective jobs she was finding. She said, "I love my job, and I love my team, but my colleagues from college are all unhappy. They continuously complain about their manager, teammates, and long hours because they jumped in it without researching anything. They just were fixated by the benefits that they get with the salary."

An important factor I always consider is, who is my reporting manager? How are they perceived in the company? Can I get along with them? Landing a job should be a win-win situation. Give yourself that consideration. Too often, people get hypnotized by the salaries and titles they are offered. Your thinking can get cloudy when there are stellar benefits, an ideal location, a cushy office, or a hefty expense account. These questions will help you apply logic to your decision, instead of blindly trusting a news article.

If you do not do your homework, and you step into a new company, you're likely to get agitated by the dysfunctions you encounter. Learn what they are ahead of time, so you can plan to cope or look elsewhere. Ask yourself if you can really do this job. Everybody should have their own seat at the table, but you have to deliver and merge with the existing situation. Are you truly up for the challenge? This is how you lead with logic when stakes are high.

Remember to ask your trusted contacts for help in grasping what you may not be able to see about yourself or future opportunities. You're in charge of securing your own accountability, and as we said in the last chapter, having people close to you offering support can make all the difference in your success--particularly when they are big picture minded.

6. NOTICE EVERYONE

When Black Lives Matter protests exploded, it was touching to see minority groups being showcased in Corporate and on a national scale. Yet in this "work from home" era, I have noticed something peculiar--there's one group that's obviously struggling. Men are complaining more than anyone! They're showing up for calls looking shoddy and exhausted. For the most part, Corporate male leaders are used to having their work lives separate from their home lives. Women have more experience managing these two worlds, but since COVID, work/life balance has been rocked for one and all. We cannot deny that Corporate men are adjusting more slowly.

You might be saying, "Oh, well. I'm sure men will survive." That's true, but if a company's priority is to generate revenue, *everyone's* challenges should be weighed as they arise. They all affect the bottom line, which still reigns supreme in Corporate America. Logically, it makes sense to have everyone's interest at heart. After all, struggle is universal.

Now that you have these six strategies to lead with logic, you'll find not only balance, but harmony in your day. When you strip away your emotional reactions to study the facts in front of you, you'll get to the point where nothing can surprise you. Politics won't faze you. The news won't take over your day. You'll see people and situations as they truly are, and not how you want them to be. This is inner freedom, critical analysis, and holistic thinking. That's how rationality wins and your patience has a chance to grow. Everything that happens can make you stronger and wiser, if you're willing to seek the lesson that's being revealed.

In the next chapter, you'll get to examine another obstacle to Corporate success--complacency. When COVID hit, it felt like the surprise of the century. Businesses all over the globe were rocked to their core. Was it their fault that their products and processes became compromised and irrelevant? Well, yes and no. Even when it seems like everything is fine, everyone needs to be challenging the norm.

CHAPTER 4

CHALLENGE
THE NORM

CHALLENGE THE NORM

"Becoming is better than being."

— Carol Dweck, Ph.D.

In the 90s, I had a big breakthrough in my career. It was when the Gulf War started and Saddam Hussein had threatened the U.S. military. Back then, I was in the military semiconductor division at Texas Instruments. Our engineering teams were all located in Houston and Dallas, which were difficult areas to protect. We wound up having to relocate the engineering team to Midland-Odessa, Texas in order to safeguard our engineering team developments. The Department of Defense approved this move, and the transition began.

This wasn't good news for any of us employees. Midland is practically in the middle of a desert! Out of 200 people in our division, only a few decided to make the move. Others left the company or looked for jobs internally. I had only been married a few years and definitely didn't want to move. I was told my leadership was needed, so I begrudgingly complied. My wife stayed back in Houston, as I set up an apartment alone in Midland. Despite having lived through so many obstacles, this one did not sit well with me at all.

To fill employee gaps, we started a hiring spree. Montana State had a lot of bright engineers, so we reached out and filled the positions with a bunch of college grads. The problem was, I was the one who had to train them. When the new hires arrived, admittedly, I just ignored them. They would come into my office, and I was so busy and fixated on my own stuff, I would send them away to do menial tasks. They would come to the lab to observe, and I'd give them a book to read. I saw them as short-term helpers and a major distraction from the work I needed to do.

One of my senior mentors, Wayne, eventually came into my office. He told me, "You cannot ignore these kids. They're your responsibility, and if you teach them properly, they're not going to deter your progress. They're going to help your future." I had no choice but to comply with Wayne's wishes.

I reluctantly gave them my attention and was floored at the response. These kids became the most productive and impressive team I had ever seen. That's not all due to my training either. To my surprise, we had hired some exceptional, young individuals. Having made the tough move together, we wound up bonding as we adjusted to this sweltering, desert town. They welcomed me into their homes and wowed me with their various capabilities on the job.

Less than a year later, we all went back to Houston. Those "kids" were now my dear friends and trusted colleagues. Had my norms and realities not been interrupted, this growth would have been delayed. Not only did I evolve as an engineer, I progressed as a teacher and a professional. The company's perception of me also changed. I was now viewed as a leader who could make sacrifices, do hard work, and build a team from scratch. This grew my rank and position, and even more so, my confidence. It was a lesson in embracing what we don't want to do and seeing what happens when your norm is challenged.

By now, you know what it means to exit the well in Corporate and to become fully immersed in the intensity of what's expected of you. In this pressure-filled environment, crises will occur, yet the gifts will inevitably arise. That's often when we find our closest contacts. With people to hold you accountable, your decisions can now be led with logic, rather than with habitual reactions. This will help you to slow down and start to challenge the norms all around you.

Surely, there are better ways of doing everything, if only we become willing to examine our worlds up close. It's one thing to nit-pick and criticize out of spite. It's another to intentionally inquire what evolution can mean both personally and professionally. That's what I hope you'll receive in this chapter. Someone needs to be brave enough to ask, "What's not working here?" Let it be you!

Here are six strategies designed to help you challenge norms, at every corner:

1. SLOW DOWN AND TAKE INVENTORY

In my Microsoft days, we would have gigantic (in-person) conferences to introduce new products and get developers in the same room to teach about our software. This became our primary platform for announcing new products. Apple, Google, Facebook, and Amazon also recognized the value of conferences, and for as long I could remember, my calendar would be full of these specialized events.

What has bothered me about these conferences was this-- when I would be standing in the middle of a conference room, it was hard to do "on-the-spot" research. This would prevent me from engaging, at times, because I wanted my questions to be informed and thoughtful. I'd have to jot down notes and follow up back at the office, which often wouldn't happen. At these in-person events, my memory would often fail me. I might recall a few people at my table—*maybe*, but otherwise, names would become a blur. Can you relate to the overwhelm? Plus, I like to absorb information at my own pace, so I'd often ask a speaker to send me their presentation. It would be a rarity when they'd follow through, but these obstacles didn't hold me back from attending numerous international conferences over the last 40 years.

As a board member of the Bellevue Chamber of Commerce, we plan several major conferences each year, based on hot topics in our community. For a technology conference in June 2020, we were anticipating 500-600 people to attend. By March, everything was falling into place, until COVID concerns closed down the city.

In a virtual meeting, we decided against postponing the event. This was a technology conference, after all. "Isn't it our job to introduce technology?" a board member asked. That settled it. We had to turn this in-person event into a virtual experience. To kick off the reinvention process, we started naming all aspects of the "typical conference" that were no longer necessary or viable.

Conference planning is notoriously tedious, and especially before COVID. First, you had to find a date that worked for everyone. That was always a small miracle in itself. Then, you had to secure a location, sign the paperwork, place a deposit, and make sure all the details were correct for food, meeting rooms, welcome bags, vendor booths, volunteers, cleaning crew, first aid, name badges, disability access, and parking passes, just to name a few.

As for the speakers, their efforts had also changed dramatically. Even though they're "on stage" for only an hour or so, the amount of preparation it would take for a speaker to arrive was often extensive--childcare, laundry, dry cleaners, packing, meals, technical assistance, traffic, airplanes, clothes shopping, printers, estheticians, hairdressers, manicurists, pet boarding, parking, Lyft, and hotels. Take all those tasks and multiply by 10-12 speakers--some of whom we would pay and reimburse for their travel/expenses.

As for the participants, it can be exhausting to schedule and attend these conferences and multiple-day events. You'd have to plan to be out of the office, arrange for travel, hotel, and transportation, and pay the price of admission. Now, with this virus, we're telling people, "Stay home and find a cozy spot. We'll give you the same information for a fraction of the cost. And instead of a few (eight-hour) days, it's now a one hour per day series of talks, spread over a few weeks. You don't have to travel. You don't have to pay for the hotel. You don't have to look good. You don't even have to show up for the speakers because everything is recorded and will be available for your review later."

With no physical location needed for our technology conference, we had eliminated a long list of duties, costs, and safety measures. With the platform now online, our speakers' expertise became more accessible and affordable. The benefits were obvious to everyone involved.

At our virtual, technology conference, I found myself noticing (and remembering) people's names on the screen. It was great because I could search their background while speakers were talking to learn about their company or subject matter. You can ask questions and pulse the room, you can engage with the speaker and have other participants' opinions, and the positives just kept coming-- speaker presentations were shared with just a click, learning was more specific for participants, and connections were made to boost people's business and position the Bellevue Chamber of Commerce favorably.

In the end, money was saved (and made) by taking it online. Companies are now presenting everything virtually, and there's just no denying the cost efficiency and reach potential. As the hosts, we thought it was just as effective as a live event, and the learning curve wasn't that bad either. Sure, it would have been nice to see in-person smiles, but not when the virus is still booming--or any time soon. Collectively, we made a gigantic leap in progress. There are industry exceptions, like factories and hands-on operations, for instance, but for the majority of service-related operations and software development, a world of opportunity has just opened.

It's my nature to seek change and ask, "Why are we doing it this way?" That question is often disruptive and inconvenient, yet it warrants consideration. You cannot trust that everything is the way it should be. What would happen if we entertained worst case scenarios more frequently? How can we stretch innovation, even when nothing appears to be broken?

In a fast-paced Corporate culture, creative thinking can be difficult to achieve. Instead of going 200 miles per hour, everyone is now moving at 5-10 miles per hour, a speed that enables us to slow down and reflect. We won't be at this extreme forever, but while we're here, let's grasp the importance of challenging the norm.

2. CONSTANTLY QUESTION

Even if you're at a pinnacle of your career, or you've just reached a significant goal, you'll want to keep raising your standards. Scrutiny can be applied to all areas of your life--health, wealth, family, friends, or faith. *Do you really need to buy that Louis Vuitton bag? Have you been drinking too much coffee or wine? Do you need more exercise? What family routines need adjusting? Are you missing the practice of relaxation or meditation? What improvements can you make in your work-from-home situation?*

Companies can apply the same introspection. At Texas Instruments in the 70s, we were the world's number one semiconductor manufacturer. Little by little, we started losing our edge to the Japanese. We knew our technology was dominant, so maybe our implementation needed to improve. We didn't know for certain. For insights, management enlisted the help of our Texas Instruments Japanese division. They had been known in the company for outperforming U.S. facilities in manufacturing quality and production.

During this time, our Quality and Device Analysis team had been reading the book *Only the Paranoid Survive* by former Intel CEO Andy Grove. It's about how to manage a company through crisis and sudden change. The book cover explains Andy's terminology: "Grove calls such a moment a Strategic Inflection Point, which can be set off by almost anything: mega-competition, a change in regulations, or a seemingly modest change in technology."1 Written in the 90s, this powerful book could not be more relevant today. When a Strategic Inflection Point hits, "business as usual" goes out the window, yet when it's managed properly, a Strategic Inflection Point can be an opportunity to win the marketplace and evolve.

Grove pointed to the fact that you cannot rely on your dominance. You have to constantly question and renovate. Luckily, Texas Instruments understood this by inviting the Japanese to help. For months, they observed how we were working and the ways in which we were communicating. They were humble and respectful, to say the least. They learned about *our way* of doing things, before introducing their improvements. When they left, they hung signs everywhere saying "Be Quiet!" This didn't mean keep your voices down.

Without getting too technical, the manufacturing department was a massive area. When we transferred electronic chipsets and substrates, they were on carriers called *boats*. These boats were transitioned from various manufacturing areas on carts, which had wheels that would shake and rattle across the floor. We had always been aware of the fragile nature of these semiconductor components, but we failed to take extra measures to maintain their integrity. None of us had a clue the boats were causing stress fractures on the substrates. As a result, our customers weren't having an optimal experience with our products. "Be Quiet" meant to cease our way of handling these components and devise a better way of transporting fragile substrates.

After streamlining our process, it took us years to regain our market position. It was another reminder to never be complacent. If questioning the norm doesn't bring fresh ideas within your company, invite outside experts to help you see what's missing. Upon receiving new data, you must allow your mind to be changed. This is the true mark of a leader and creative pioneer.

Remember that innovation doesn't require you to create something new. It's about discovering weaknesses in current processes and products, and finding an upgrade. Case in point: Amazon gets credit for inventing at-home delivery, but it was the milkman back in the mid-1900 who invented home delivery. The only difference between that guy and the Amazon driver is the personal connection people would make with the milkman. Today, there's no need for Amazon to perpetuate that doorstep relationship. We're connected to thousands of people virtually across the globe.

Uber, Lyft, and bicycle delivery services are also positioned as innovators, but it's always been customary in other countries to share rides and use motorcycles and bikes for deliveries. Same with Airbnb--when traveling, it would be stressful to find no occupancy in hotels. There have always been people who've rented out rooms to those in need. I mention this not to discard the progress these companies have made, but rather to demonstrate how these companies put an app around common conveniences.

3. ADOPT A GROWTH MINDSET

Years ago, I read a book called *'Mindset'* by world-renowned Stanford University psychologist Carol S. Dweck. She used decades of research to illustrate how success in school, work, sports, arts, and almost every area of human endeavor can be dramatically influenced by how we think about our talents and abilities. Her book description reads, "People with a *fixed mindset*—those who believe that abilities are fixed—are less likely to flourish than those with a *growth mindset*—those who believe that abilities can be developed."

In 2016, Microsoft invited Dr. Dweck to their campus. Having had first-hand experience with Microsoft leaders suffering from a fixed mindset, I couldn't help but recall how it would hamper our progress and cause subsequent delay in product delivery and market loss. Nothing could penetrate some people's fixed beliefs and standard operations. I found that infuriating. Dr. Dweck gave a thrilling talk encouraging employees to apply growth mindset to their daily work habits. Her advice was both quickly implemented and instantly effective.

The problem of fixed mindset often goes undetected, particularly with company leaders. I can remember interviewing a candidate from inside the company to join our team. This person came highly recommended, and had a proven track record and unique expertise. After rounds of interviews, I introduced him to our department head for final approval. This senior leader refused to proceed with the interview. His exact words were "I don't think this guy adds value to our team." Clearly, his fixed mindset did not allow him to believe an engineer's capabilities could be developed.

Even worse, this leader was the final decision maker in our hiring and all major decisions for that division. Needless to say, the candidate went ahead and accepted a position in another group and enjoyed a thriving career.

When I hit this roadblock in Corporate, I can remember being frustrated that nobody was challenging this guy's fixed mindset. This led me to intentionally create work environments where people's assumptions could be challenged as a normal daily activity. This way, it wouldn't be as painful. With this foundation, we could ask why more often and disrupt the status quo without bruising egos.

4. TAKE OWNERSHIP OF ERRORS

History is filled with product inventions that came about due to wrong science, an accidental stumble, or a blatant mistake--the inventions of penicillin, Post-it Notes, and plastics, to name a few. In my organizations, I always tell the team that I want to be the first to know about mistakes. I don't want to hear it on the news or from someone outside of the company. Bring it to me. We might even discover something good from the error. Not addressing mistakes at the early stage makes the error more costly and difficult to resolve. It also breaks trust between people. I encourage my team to be transparent. Don't hide anything. Face your shortcomings.

In the 80s, I was assigned to a complex, large-scale project that stretched my knowledge and capabilities. I had to comprehend numerous components of a computational platform, then design a chipset to incorporate all those components to test our prototype. This involved careful collaboration between our engineering teams. After months of working hard, designing reviews, traveling between facilities, adopting techniques, and operating machinery, my work was submitted to manufacturing. This was to be my first chip design. I waited nervously to receive the product. Weeks went by before I found out it had failed.

I was disappointed and panicked, but I wouldn't let myself wallow there. Without saying a word to anyone, I figured out why it didn't work and sent it back to manufacturing for correction. That was the easy part. Next, I wrote a detailed memo to my colleagues and managers explaining what I'd done. As a junior in the company, I braced for what might come next, although a weight had been lifted by publicly confessing. I just wanted them to know it was my mistake, and that I had learned from it and did my best to correct it.

In Martial Arts, this is how you progress. It was the only way I knew how to cope.

Can you believe management appreciated what I had done? They didn't look at it as a failure. They saw it as me solving the problem with remarkable speed. They did not correlate the mistake to me. They credited me with the solution. I was surprised to have been put on a pedestal and later promoted. Our division leader even traveled from headquarters to thank me. I remember feeling speechless at that moment. This set the course for me to challenge tough problems, put my fear aside, and constantly address the problems and issues that no one else has taken on. Taking ownership for my errors has seeped into every aspect of my life.

Imagine a world where political and business leaders would adopt this mentality and practice. We, as a society, might not be so hard on ourselves and each other. We must break the norm of hiding errors, trying to justify them, and placing blame on others. Heck, when things fall apart, everyone knows whose fault it was anyway. In the end, that person will not survive in the Corporate world if they cannot find peace in being openly imperfect.

My mentees and even my kids' friends sometimes call me in tears when they've made a mistake. To them, it's the end of the world. They think their whole career is over. I laugh and try to help them find some levity. "Come on. Mistakes are part of being human. If you don't make mistakes, you're not trying hard enough." When given the truth of a situation, it's fun to watch them bounce right back.

In this COVID era, your mistakes might be a little more private, since the entire office isn't there to witness your failing. Still, own your mistake, not just as a display of humility, but for the learning opportunity it provides you and others. This gives everybody a chance to understand how different brains, backgrounds, and levels perceive the subject at hand. Plus, if mistakes are discovered early, it will cost you much less. You either pay now or pay later. You either do it great now, or you do it over. Nelson Mandela said, "I never lose. I either win or learn." That's a helpful mantra for work and life.

IF YOU DON'T MAKE MISTAKES, YOU'RE NOT TRYING HARD ENOUGH

5. ASK STUPID QUESTIONS

When I invite people to brainstorm an idea, the first thing I say is, "If you don't ask stupid questions, you will not be invited back." People laugh, and I have to keep going, "No, it's true. If you don't ask a stupid question, our dialogue will not be productive. I want new solutions, I want innovation, and if you're not here for that, why do I need you?"

I did not always practice this mindset. I embraced it from one of our brilliant senior leaders at Microsoft in the early stages of my career. I had been invited to a brainstorming session with a few of my colleagues for the next version of Microsoft Office. Needless to say, I was thrilled to be invited and to participate in this elite group of talented people. The first thing Steven Sinofsky, our Senior Vice President of Office Product Development, said was, "If you don't ask stupid questions, you will not be invited back." At the time I didn't comprehend the remark and to cut the story short, I wasn't invited to future sessions.

Asking a stupid question takes vulnerability. It's viewed as a risk because it could reveal your lack of understanding. In my startups and company, my primary goal is to encourage failures and mistakes. They provide the best learning for everyone involved. A task can be described in extensive detail, yet unless we fail and make mistakes, how will we ever progress?

In a capitalistic culture, when you screw up, say something wrong, or have a bad day, the "gossip train" will wonder what's going on with you. Instead of cowering in shame, stand up and proclaim your error. State what you just learned. We're told to stay inside the lines, but this prevents transformation. I cannot stress this enough. Rather than seeking perfection and promotions, show up and be genuinely curious. Risk embarrassing yourself, for the sake of normalizing it.

I pride myself in being someone who will ask a bold or clarifying question. In fact, I've built my career on it--not only by being a disruptor, but also positioning myself as having a genuine desire to learn. I'm not there to stir the pot or slow things down. People can tell from my tone of voice and positioning that I am sincerely interested in broadening my knowledge. During my Microsoft years, Bill Gates would model this brilliantly. If you're presenting to him, you better be prepared for his piercing questions.

Do you know the famous Einstein saying, "If you can't explain it simply, you don't understand it well enough?" I can remember preparing for weeks just to stand in front of Bill. Our goal was to be as clear and concise as possible, otherwise, that weakness would be exposed. To prepare for those meetings, to prepare for *anything* important, we had to reject the notion that asking questions of each other was disrespectful or a sign of stupidity. It became essential to our success. No question was off the table!

After several interactions with Bill, we realized those weeks of preparations were critical. He would put you on the spot, and at times was very tough. Not for the sake of embarrassing you, but he simply wanted to understand the issue and the solution that was presented to him. He would leave no stone unturned.

Offering clarity and having a firm understanding of everyone's expectations, including deadlines and objectives, are of prime importance right now. When the project is complete, there won't be surprises. People want to feel safe while doing business. You have a chance to lead by having thorough communication and the willingness to challenge people's assumptions and unspoken fears.

As you begin to forge new connections, surround yourself with people who will ask both stupid and tough questions.

There are ways to pose questions so they don't sound insulting or aggressive. Position yourself as wanting to learn, rather than criticize, so when you ask your questions, they serve to help everyone gain understanding. It also helps presenters better define what they are trying to present.

It's all in your delivery of the question. People who do this well generally are not conflict avoidant. They can step into discomfort and without getting rattled. These are the leaders to watch. Emulate their style and use tough questions to open doors to your future—and to know which ones to close as well.

6. GO THE EXTRA MILE

Master Chang would teach basic and advanced Martial Arts, but certain techniques were held close like secret family recipes. Kung Fu masters, he said, would never teach their best techniques. After all, it was a matter of life and death in those times--students could use those lethal techniques against them. The only way to learn these lethal techniques was to challenge the Grandmasters by taking your life into your hands. One example of this treacherous behavior was when somebody who is really eager to learn a technique will go to that Grandmaster's home, knock on the door, and start using all sorts of obscenities for the master to come out and beat him. If he survives, he learns a coveted technique. That's how sacred wisdom travels from master to master. It's an unbelievable way to learn--the grit of that society! And then we look at American culture and see how everything is handed to us, and very few take advantage. The norm is to take what's handed to you.

In Corporate, you have to seek out the information you need and be relentless. You have to fully commit yourself. Those Martial Arts "masters in training" risked dying to learn something. Corporate isn't asking for your life, but rather asking for your genuine hunger. You need to go the extra mile to learn. A few of my mentees who live across U.S. borders are graduate students at various universities in Europe and the Middle East. They beg me to send them information that they cannot access in their countries. Very often, I send them old books and publications for their review. They're eager and thirsty for knowledge that they cannot access themselves. Corporate success demands a similar tenacity.

Growth of any kind gets delayed when we refrain from asking what needs to change. When you need to challenge the status quo, turn to the strategies in this chapter. Remember to slow down and reflect on what else is possible. This might mean you ask a silly question or make an obvious mistake. These behaviors should be welcomed. Don't stop questioning. Adopt a growth mindset. That is how we transform as people. It's what we need in business to advance innovation and humanize our experience.

In the next chapter, you'll learn how to keep balance when the world around you is topsy turvy. Chaos and change don't have to kill you. Long hours and Corporate pressure don't have to become your norm. There's an avenue for greater self-care that's available to one and all.

CHAPTER 5

DON'T LOSE YOUR BALANCE

DON'T LOSE
YOUR BALANCE

"Balance is not something you find, it's something you create."

— Jana Kingsford

When I think back on some of my more difficult days in Corporate, I can recall my friends and colleagues going through stress-related emergencies--heart attacks, anxiety attacks, and even suicides. At Texas Instruments and Microsoft, the unrelenting pressure of delivery, timelines, and management would inevitably overwhelm. We'd have ambulances come into our workplace on a daily basis, followed by a message saying that "so and so" had been taken to the hospital.

This would always happen during our products' "ship cycle." That's when a product reaches maturity and is ready to be released to the market. It was a stressful time, to say the least. Families knew not to disturb or ask for much during the ship cycle. We'd miss vacations, birthdays, and kids' sporting events. Those limitations had to be accepted by us and our families, or there would be hell to pay both at home and work. These are some of the downsides you have to accept with Corporate.

As I talk to people today with remote work being prevalent, they say the intensity of Corporate is pretty much the same. Sure, it's better for some because you can cope while at home, but the shift to virtual business hasn't lessened the pressure on Corporate employees. So how do you take good care of yourself? How do you find that elusive balance?

Work/life balance is one of the most talked about areas in Corporate culture, but not many practice it. We discuss it at length, similar to diversity, equality, and inclusion, but progress is minimal. We read books on this topic and hold conferences to promote it. We even train employees on it, but we keep missing the boat somehow. We continually get unbalanced out of fear of loss and inadequacy.

In the first four chapters, we talked about fine-tuning your mindset to better cope and succeed in Corporate environments. This will help you challenge norms and use logic to drive your decisions. You also now understand how to face crisis and controversy as an opportunity to bond with people and evolve as a person. To close out this book, let's now revisit the Prologue.

Remember the high-powered business guy versus the humble fisherman? Each one of them had achieved their own form of utopia, but the businessman's route to success lacked focus on health, family, friends, rest, and hobbies. So far, the bulk of this book has placed us in the life of the businessman. Now, it's time to learn how to fish. In Corporate, particularly if you're working remotely, you now have a chance to become the fisherman--to set boundaries and definitions of what balance and joy mean to you. You can vacillate between executive and fisherman, but it takes intentional planning and thought to find the sweet spot.

Here are five strategies that will help you structure your life and work for greater balance.

1. CLAIM YOUR HIDDEN DREAMS

When I was growing up, nearly everyone I knew followed the societal routine of college, marriage, children, and the purchase of a home in suburbia. These traditions were passed down from family and friends, and were presented as positive directions that most of us tried to mimic. The same is true with our careers. We were told there's a vertical ladder to climb. If we worked hard and proved our worth, we'd get raises, bonuses, and promotions, until our titles grew in importance. Because of this, older generations had one primary model to follow. This stifled people's imaginations for what was truly possible for themselves. Beyond that, it kept people continually striving and stressing: *Why haven't I been promoted yet? When am I going to get my next raise? Why did that person get chosen before me? Should I be looking for bigger jobs elsewhere?*

In this final chapter, please realize that COVID has released you from having to engineer both your life and career based on outdated expectations. The old ways of life have officially died. Unconventional has never been more accepted and possible. If you aren't feeling alive with curiosity about what life could bring you next, you're missing an invitation to stretch your imagination during this virtual era. There's never been a better time to get serious about the career and lifestyle you never thought you could have. It's also important to note what you cannot live without. Allow me to explain further.

In the first few months of COVID, when we only left home for the grocery store, it became clear just how fast paced our lives had truly been. Our old habits were up for scrutiny, and we longed for what we had to leave behind. We missed eating at restaurants, getting haircuts, going to the gym, visiting friends, shopping at stores, and traveling to our favorite places. On the flipside, we were also able to see how we were living unsustainably and in excess. Busy had become the accepted norm.

The quest for more, more, more is a natural result of living in a capitalist culture. Capitalism dictates that the more you work, the more money you'll make, the better life you will have, the better house you get, the better car you'll be able to own. The more you work, the more you can provide for your family. So you work harder and start cutting down on the people, places, and things that truly matter. Your eye remains on goals that require you to work harder and harder, yet other parts of your life begin to slowly slip away. It's easy to fall into this rhythm.

COVID taught us how to find our basic needs again. For instance, I was visiting a large corporation yesterday and ran into a manager friend. I asked, "What are you doing here?" He replied, "It's better for me to be here. It really is. Working from home was like being in solitary confinement." My friend now understands he needs to be at the office for productivity and inner harmony. It might be different for you. You might actually love working from home, but your "non-negotiable" might be having to help with housework or getting to a yoga class each day. You might have realized how much you need to be in nature, or how much you love not getting dressed up for work. Now that these basic needs have been revealed, don't ever lose sight of them again. You've been given knowledge about what you require to feel your best. Why not find jobs and opportunities that will honor those personal wishes?

Pre-COVID, most people looked for jobs that were close to them in proximity. Corporate America gave priority to U.S. applicants. Relocation costs played a major role in hiring practices. From state to state, city to city, the costs are fairly minimal, however, to move international talent would involve visas, paperwork, and other financial hassles. Today, when U.S. companies are looking for talent, they're interviewing people in Europe, India, or China. This is an amazing opportunity for both employer and employee to diversify the workforce and welcome fresh thinking. It's also a great time to fulfill any dreams you have of working overseas. *Have you always wanted to live in another country, but you couldn't leave your job? Would you love to study with an innovator overseas?*

Let this time of mass transformation guide you to your dream scenarios. Like the fisherman, you get to define how this looks and feels. Get honest about what you want and be persistent in making it happen. As always, do the homework, do the math, and let logic guide your next moves, but don't be afraid to dream big and go for it.

2. LEARN WHAT BALANCE MEANS ELSEWHERE

America always strives to become the most innovative and productive nation, but the carnage of this endeavor is what you might imagine. Those who are driving these advancements get burned out, depressed, and restless. Other countries don't operate this way. I learned this firsthand while working in international product development at our Microsoft Office in France. In 2009, I arrived there on the weekend and was at headquarters on Monday, Tuesday, Wednesday. On Thursday at 10 AM, Microsoft Campus Security came in and while speaking French, they escorted me off campus. I kept asking what's going on. They said, "You must leave. You have to go." I grabbed my laptop and went back to the hotel, frantically trying to contact my manager, who wound up being on vacation. I had to wait in my hotel and do my work without going back to the office. My mind raced. "Did I do something wrong? Have I been fired? Did I get laid off?" When I finally connected with my manager in the U.S., he couldn't understand why they made me leave either. It took him until Monday morning to discover what protocol I had broken. Turns out, I had worked more than 35 hours that week, and by Thursday at 10 AM, I had worked more than 40 hours, which is breaking the law. To let me continue would have caused serious problems for the company.

So in Europe, there are well defined guidelines for workers. They tell you what kind of work/balance to have. And if you're laid off by a big corporation, it's actually like hitting the jackpot. I didn't realize this until I had international employees. At Texas Instruments in the 1990s, I had six people on my semiconductor manufacturing team in Germany. Layoffs had begun and my instinct was to fight to keep certain team members. Hans was about 50 years old at the time. He was reliable and experienced, and when I was able to save his job, he wasn't very happy with me. Over beers, he told me, "Next time, don't do me any favors." He explained that when U.S. companies lay off an employee in Europe, the incentives are so immense, you barely need to work. I had no idea!

Unlike the U.S., balance is well defined in Europe. That's why you see a very clear gap between the productivity that comes out of U.S. borders versus theirs. Our lack of balance makes us a leading nation in technology and innovation. European advancements aren't as plentiful, but the people are generally more balanced. As you consider overseas opportunities or do business with people overseas, seek to discover what kind of work/life balances have been established.

3. DETERMINE YOUR BOUNDARIES

During quarantine, I've watched my Corporate kids struggle for balance and boundaries. At 5:45 PM, a manager would call and say, "Hey, can you do this one quick thing?" Then, an email would arrive, and it was one thing after the other. When they finally stood up from their desks, it was 7:30 PM. They would emerge into the kitchen or living room unlively and exhausted.

Corporate isn't going to create balance for you, nor is your manager. It would be nice if leaders modeled and enforced good boundaries and work/life balance, but they feel pressure, too, and will react by stretching everyone's capabilities. It's up to you to know your limitations, understand the situation, and guard your free time by developing boundaries to alleviate tension and pressure.

My son and I were headed to a game Friday night and had plans together for Saturday as well. On Friday morning, his manager called asking for several items to be completed

ASAP. Our father/son plans were scrapped immediately, as Baabak didn't want to say no to his boss. After all, he's still a junior in his role and learning the ropes.

I tell my kids and mentees that management will take advantage of you, as much as you let them. They will bend you until you crack. It's up to you to show them your limitations. You can say things like, "I will not be checking email from 7 PM - 7 AM," and that's fine, if you're able to get your tasks done in your window of productivity. Like we mentioned earlier, you have to get honest with yourself about what you're truly capable of achieving and where you could use some help.

Okay, now you might be asking, "What if they pile work on me at the last minute?" Well, that is a given. When you want to say no, but you don't know if you can, stop and assess if the work you've been asked to do will slow down progress if not done immediately. Is it a show stopper for your product, customers, or other teams? If it isn't, I schedule the work appropriately and either delegate to my team or complete it myself. If it's a priority and time dependent, I address it based on its urgency, but communicate with my manager and team members in regards to delays on other tasks.

It's likely you're sitting there thinking, "Wait a minute. When I say no to tasks, shame is thrown my way!" Yes, I know what you mean. Microsoft prides itself on hiring very smart people. If you cannot do what needs to be done, you will be reminded that smarter people can and will replace you. There's always that looming threat of realizing someone else could pull off what you're incapable of achieving in 40+ hours per week. This pressure will always be there, but don't forget to stand in your confidence and state your boundaries when it's possible to use them.

4. CONFIDENCE = KNOW YOUR STRENGTHS & WEAKNESSES

Rebecca Minkoff established the Female Founder Collective and is a social media influencer. She writes, "There are endless formulas about how to be confident. My experience has taught me it's much simpler: Confidence is about being yourself and feeling comfortable in your skin."[1]

Being comfortable in your skin means you have to know your limitations and weaknesses, so they can be property managed. Feeling comfortable in your skin requires self-knowledge. Without those insights into what makes you exceptional *and* vulnerable, you open yourself to unpleasant surprises that can be detrimental to your career.

At an executive leadership talk at Microsoft, Bill Gates once openly discussed why he fired one of his top developers. Everybody had been questioning him on this decision, including HR and the rest of the development team. Bill stood firmly behind his decision. Although this guy was an amazing developer, he wasn't good at working with the team. He was working on his own areas of interest and on his own timeline. Each day, we had to get this developer back on track with the team. "So what good is being the best, when you're not doing what the corporation needs?" He was right. You can be incredibly skilled in your job, but if you don't know your weaknesses and work hard to overcome them, you will run the risk of getting fired. Understand your strengths and apply them in a proper forum.

Can you adapt to what's needed of you? You can't be too proud of what you bring to the table if you're not able to deliver as others have requested. Believe me, people are noticing your weaknesses. Stay ahead of the curve and prove that you're actively working to resolve them, so you can show up as your best.

In Martial Arts, you learn how to use your strengths to cover your weaknesses. Everyone has a stronger and weaker side of the body. If the left side is weaker, you use your stronger right side to protect your left. Similarly, when you work in a corporation, it's your job to manage your weaknesses. If your weak side is being shy, then maybe you shouldn't be leading teams. If your strong side is being analytical, you might not be great at brainstorming. You must learn how and where your strengths can get magnified and weaknesses can be controlled.

Master Chang had a hidden trick to mask his deficiencies. At gyms, he would often wow us by lifting random weights above his head with ease. As his students, we would try to match his confidence and success, but would embarrass ourselves by failing to get the weight above our chest. One day, my Sifu, John, pulled me to the side of the gym and said, "One must not embarrass himself in public. You're a black belt and one of the most senior members of this team. If you seem unsure with your actions in public, your vulnerability will be too apparent."

He said, "Master Chang doesn't think like that because it's a show of weakness. When he raises the weight above his head and drops it, it's a demonstration of his strength. But let me tell you a secret. Look at Master Chang's feet when no one is watching him. He is testing that weight with his feet to determine his ability to lift it. Only when he is one hundred percent sure he can pick it up will he make the attempt, as all eyes will fall upon him."

This discovery about Master Chang grew my respect for him as a person and teacher, and it explained why he never got into a fight that he could not win. After all, everybody needs assurance from their leader. When Corporate intensity starts to peak, confident leaders help us achieve balance. The lesson here is to be in control of your own situation, as much as you can, along with knowing your capabilities and limitations.

5. REDEFINE "GOOD DAY"

What would your ideal day of work be like? What would work/life balance look like for you? For me, it's about maintaining a daily routine that starts early in the morning. Weather (and COVID) permitting, I go biking or exercise at the local indoor club, followed by a few minutes of relaxation in a jacuzzi or steam room. During this time, I plan the rest of the day. In my 40+ year career, I've found that morning movement and contemplation are essential to starting my day on a positive note.

Having discipline makes me feel calm. Perhaps that's influenced by my love for Martial Arts. I always say, if you wake up in the morning, make your bed, brush your teeth, and get started on your chores, you're going to survive in Corporate better than the person who doesn't make their bed. Not everyone is programmed to be like this, but those who are have a much easier time. Employing a military-like discipline, especially now that remote work is prevalent, is essential to finding balance. Without structure and discipline to your day, success is hard to accomplish.

Another trick I use to ensure balance is to close out the day by assessing how I did--Did I eat healthy? Did I get fresh air and exercise? Did I give to family and friends? Did I do my daily chores? Did I get my work done on time? Was I a positive force in my community? Did I have any quiet time? If there's a major deficiency in one or more categories, I don't beat myself up, although I also don't label it a "good day." That doesn't mean it was bad, it means a good day is one that is balanced, similar to the fisherman. When good days become your priority, you won't look at discipline as something that limits you. You will see it as a key element in your mental and physical well-being, an attitude adjuster that has a ripple effect out in the world.

Mandy Hale said, "A great attitude becomes a great day, which becomes a great month, which becomes a great year, which becomes a great life."[2] By seeking balance, your attitude can be fed a variety of experiences where you both give and receive. It starts by claiming your hidden dreams. Now that COVID has destroyed conventional thinking, what are you longing to do? Once you have determined your basic needs and desires, investigate what it means to find balance there. This will help you set boundaries with confidence, knowing you are aware of the big picture, as well as your strengths and weaknesses.

IN CLOSING . . .

As a perpetual student and grateful participant in Corporate America, it has been a joy sharing what I've learned from my teachers and mentors. Now that you've heard my stories and philosophies, my fellow students, Corporate America doesn't have to be so exhausting. That doesn't mean you won't be tired. We all feel wiped out from time to time. It means you'll be able to find balance without sacrificing your potential for success, and at the end of your life, you won't regret the losses along the way because they will also be met with plenty of meaningful moments.

It is not easy, but if you are willing to see the Corporate world as it really is, you will discover your power to learn, grow, and achieve. It doesn't really matter who you know or how hard you work. Your ability to thrive depends on understanding Corporate politics, culture, and the purpose of working in a capitalistic society.

You're now equipped to stand strong in the face of criticism and change, knowing they will always lead to greater self-awareness, stronger connections, and further innovation. You now have philosophies to enter this pressure-filled, money-focused terrain without losing your sanity. You're now prepared for anything, and if surprises rattle your confidence, you know how to seek logic and follow it religiously.

Corporate is not for everyone, but if you are willing to adopt everyday practices of balance and discipline when you are pushed to excel, the rewards will be plentiful. You will contribute to cutting-edge advancements, you'll make a healthy income, and you'll know how to develop a better version of yourself during every phase of your career. All you need to do is look in the mirror and see whose face appears. If you don't see the fisherman, you now know how to summon him back, along with the peace and balance his spirit brings.

ABOUT THE AUTHOR

Michael Nassirian started his career at Texas Instruments in 1983 and later moved to Microsoft, holding leadership positions for nearly two decades. With a proven track record for disruptive technologies, Michael played a major role at Microsoft in developing the HoloLens. In 2016, he established ARVR Academy, where young talents and entrepreneurs learn about the world of Augmented and Virtual Reality technology. ARVR Academy provides tools, training, and resources to implement cutting-edge ideas into the business world, including cyber security, fiber optics, and Big Data.

Michael lives in Bellevue, Washington with his wife and two kids and is dedicated to community service and involvement. He's an active member of the Bellevue, Washington Rotary

Club, Bellevue Chamber of Commerce, National Multiple Sclerosis Society, and the East Hub non-profit Performing Arts organization.

END NOTES

CHAPTER 1

1. Salvador Rodriguez, "Zuckerberg Says Employees Moving out of Silicon Valley May Face Pay Cuts," CNBC, May 21, 2020, https://www.cnbc.com/2020/05/21/zuckerberg-50percent-of-facebook-employees-could-be-working-remotely.html.

2. Rodriguez.

3. Taylor Soper, "Amazon Hires 248,500 People in Q3 as Jeff Bezos Challenges Large Employers to Raise Minimum Wage," GeekWire, October 29, 2020, https://www.geekwire.com/2020/amazons-hires-248500-people-q3-jeff-bezos-challenges-large-employers-raise-minimum-wage/.

CHAPTER 3

1. Jodi Kantor and David Streitfeld, "Inside Amazon: Wrestling Big Ideas in a Bruising Workplace - The New York Times," The New York Times, August 15, 2015, https://www.nytimes.com/2015/08/16/technology/inside-amazon-wrestling-big-ideas-in-a-bruising-workplace.html.

2. Joe Nocera, "Jeff Bezos and the Amazon Way," The New York Times, August 21, 2015, https://www.nytimes.com/2015/08/22/opinion/joe-nocera-jeff-bezos-and-the-amazon-way.html.

CHAPTER 4

1. Andrew S. Grove, Only the Paranoid Survive: How to Exploit the Crisis Points That Challenge Every Company (New York: Currency Doubleday, 1999), back cover.

2. Carol Dweck, Mindset: Changing the Way You Think to Fulfil Your Potential, 6th Edition (New York: Robinson, 2017), back cover.

CHAPTER 5

1. Rebecca Minkoff, "The Simple Truth I've Learned About Confidence | LinkedIn," LinkedIn, October 8, 2020, https://www.linkedin.com/pulse/simple-truth-ive-learned-confidence-rebecca-minkoff/.

2. Mandy Hale (@TheSingleWoman), "A Great Attitude Becomes a Great Day Which Becomes a Great Month Which Becomes a Great Year Which Becomes a Great LIFE :)," Twitter, February 5, 2013, https://twitter.com/TheSingleWoman/status/298679992244645888.